中英双语

第一辑

THE FALCON'S FEATHERS
游隼的羽毛

[美] 罗恩·罗伊 著
[美] 约翰·史蒂文·格尼 绘 刘巧丽 译

湖南少年儿童出版社
·长沙·

人物介绍

丁丁

三人小组的成员，聪明勇敢，喜欢读推理小说，紧急关头总能保持头脑冷静。喜欢在做事之前好好思考！

乔希

三人小组的成员，活泼机智，喜欢吃好吃的食物，常常有意想不到的点子。

露丝

三人小组的成员，活泼开朗，喜欢从头到脚穿同一种颜色的衣服，总是那个能找到大部分线索的人。

环境保护部的工作人员，接到孩子们的电话后，去森林里寻找游隼。

库尔特

兽医，孩子们发现游隼之后，亨利帮小游隼做了检查，并将它收留在兽医诊所治疗。

亨利医生

格蕾丝·洛克伍德

亨利医生的助手，细心地照料着兽医诊所的动物，因为一些巧合的疑点，被三人组怀疑是偷走游隼的嫌疑人。

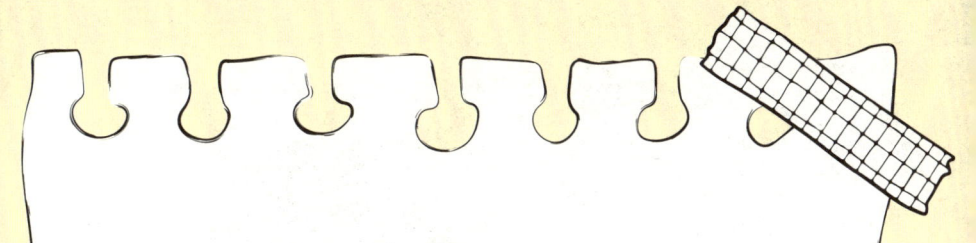

字母 F 代表 frightened，害怕……

一只棕色的小鸟蜷缩在杂草中。它的喙很锋利，一双黑眼睛闪闪发亮。

"是一只游隼！"乔希说，"这肯定是鸟巢里的游隼！"

…………

"这只可怜的小家伙看起来好像很害怕。"露丝说。

乔希脱下 T 恤，将它小心翼翼地盖在小鸟的身上。"如果它看不到我们，就不会那么害怕了。"乔希解释道。他将被 T 恤包着的小鸟抱在胸前。

"我们应该怎么安置它呢？"丁丁问。

"我们把它带到翁太太那里吧！"露丝说。

"嘿，这是什么？"乔希一边说着，一边轻轻地拉出游隼的一条腿。

游隼的腿上缠着一条细细的金属带子。

第一章

丁丁踩到了一根树枝,树枝断裂发出一声脆响。

"天哪,丁丁,听起来你笨拙得像头大象!"乔希说,"我们必须保持安静!"

"乔希·平托,你要带我们去哪里?"露丝问,"我浑身都是划痕!你为什么不告诉我们要

穿过有刺的灌木丛?"

孩子们已经在树林深处,但离马路不是太远。高高的树木下,灌木丛长得十分茂密。

乔希咧着嘴对他的朋友们笑。"这是个惊喜。"他说,"相信我,你们会喜欢这个惊喜的。"

"哼,我可不喜欢这些蚊子。"丁丁咕哝着。

露丝坐在一根圆木上,挠着脚踝上的一个包。"我不走了,除非你说出你的秘密。"她说。

"我也不走了。"丁丁说着,扑通一声坐到露丝身边,"说吧,乔希。你为什么要把我们拉进这个树林?"

"而且那个双筒望远镜是干什么用的?"露丝问。

"好吧,我告诉你们。"乔希挤到他们两个中间坐了下来,然后从口袋里拿出一张纸。他把纸在他的膝盖上摊开。

上面画着一只鸟。它的羽毛是深色的,喙是弯的,眼睛下面还有黑色的标记。

"这是什么?"丁丁问,"一只鹰?"

乔希摇了摇头。"不,这是一只游隼。游隼

几乎要灭绝了,但是现在绿地镇里有一窝!"

丁丁顿时倍感钦佩。"这是你画的吗?"

乔希点了点头。"是的。我发现了一个鸟巢,里面有三只小游隼。我已经观察它们好几周了。"

"而你今天才告诉我们?"露丝说,"真是谢谢你的分享呢,乔希。"

乔希将那幅画折好,塞进口袋。"游隼不喜欢被人打扰,"他说,"我想等那三只小游隼长大一些再告诉你们。"

丁丁抬头看了看那些树。"所以,那个鸟巢在哪里?"他问。

乔希站了起来。"我们就快到了。"他说。

孩子们在灌木丛中摸索着前进。透过一些枝丫,丁丁瞥见了印第安河。

一会儿,乔希停下了脚步。"就在那里,"他小声说,"就在那边空地上的那棵高高的树上。"

"我只看到了树叶。"露丝说。

乔希指向树腰的位置。"看见枯枝上面那团棕色的东西了吗?"

"我看见了!"露丝大叫了一声。

"我也看见了。"丁丁说,"你是怎么爬上去的?"

"我没有爬上去,"乔希说,"如果你惊动了鸟巢里的鸟,鸟爸爸和鸟妈妈可能会抛弃它们的宝宝。"

乔希指着空地边缘的一棵白桦树,说:"我爬上了那棵树,然后用双筒望远镜看的。"

"我们能爬上去看一看吗?"露丝问。

"当然可以。"乔希说,"但是我们必须保持安静!我不想吓到它们。"

白桦树很好爬,光滑的树干就像一个天然的梯子。丁丁和露丝跟着乔希爬上了一根粗壮的树枝。

乔希举着他的双筒望远镜看向另一棵树。他转动两个目镜之间的小转轮,调整焦距。

"太奇怪了。"他小声嘀咕着。

"怎么奇怪了?"露丝问。

"让我看看。"丁丁拿过望远镜,透过镜片眯着眼睛看。从他的位置看过去,可以直接看到鸟

A to Z 神秘案件

巢。鸟巢是用小树枝、松针和枯叶筑成的。但是里面没有游隼。丁丁只看到几根羽毛。他扬起眉毛看着乔希。

"它们去哪儿了?"他问。

"怎么了?"露丝问。

乔希看着她说:"小游隼们不见了。"

第二章

"也许它们飞走了。"露丝说。

孩子们爬下来,站在鸟巢所在的那棵树下。

乔希摇了摇头。"它们才刚刚开始学飞,"他说,"还没准备好离开它们的父母呢。"

"它们会不会掉下来了?"丁丁问完,看了一眼地面。

"我觉得不会。"乔希说,"如果它们掉下来了,它们的爸爸妈妈会在这里看着它们的。"

他眉头紧蹙。"我觉得是什么东西带走了那

些小游隼。"他说。

"什么意思?"露丝问,"是什么东西?"

"某种动物。"乔希解释道,"猫头鹰和蛇就喜欢吃鸟宝宝。"

"但是小游隼的父母不会保护它们吗?"丁丁问。

"当然会了。"乔希说,"除非它们的父母也发生了某种意外。"

"也许有什么东西把它们的父母吓跑了。"露丝说。

乔希摇了摇头。"父母不会丢下它们的孩子。"

"那它们还会遇到什么事?"丁丁问,"五只游隼不会就这么消失了!"

"我不知道。"乔希说道。他看起来很担心。"快走吧,我们出去。我想将这件事报告上去。"

"向谁报告?"露丝问。她和丁丁跟着乔希沿着道路往回走。

"我也不确定。但是我们可以去问问翁太太。"乔希说,"她知道很多关于动物的事情。"

二十分钟后,孩子们到了翁太太开的毛脚宠

17

A to Z 神秘案件

物店。她正在清理一个大大的金鱼缸。

"嘿，孩子们。"翁太太说，"有什么事吗？我准备打烊了。"

游隼的羽毛

乔希向她说明了游隼失踪的事。"它们昨天还在那里,"他说,"今天就不见了!"

翁太太在她的牛仔裤上擦了擦手。"那确实很奇怪。"她说。

"游隼是一种濒危动物，"乔希说，"我应该向谁报告这件事吗？"

"这主意不错，乔希。"翁太太说。她走向桌子那边，拉开一个抽屉。

"给你。"她一边说着，一边递给乔希一张卡片，"这是环境保护部——简称DEP——的电话号码。他们在消防站那边有个办公室。"

"谢谢您，翁太太。"乔希说，"我可以用一下您的电话吗？"

翁太太回去继续清理金鱼缸时，乔希拨打了卡片上的电话号码。

丁丁和露丝在旁边听着乔希向电话那边的人说明发现鸟巢和游隼失踪的事。最后，他感谢了和他通话的那个人，挂掉了电话。

"有人会去那里看一看。"他对丁丁和露丝说，"但刚刚和我通话的那个人说，很可能是猫头鹰叼走了小游隼。"

露丝耸了耸肩膀，说："可怜的游隼们！"

孩子们向翁太太道谢后就离开了宠物店。

外面天渐渐黑了。露丝、乔希和丁丁穿过主

游隼的羽毛

街，走过中心公园。一群鸭子正在池塘里游水。鸭爸爸和鸭妈妈注意到有人来了后，大声地向它们的宝宝嘎嘎地叫了起来。小鸭子们也迅速游向它们的爸爸妈妈。

乔希停下脚步，说："我不觉得一只猫头鹰能带走那些小游隼。"

"你认为不能？"丁丁问。

乔希摇了摇头。"游隼爸爸和游隼妈妈都很凶！它们不会让猫头鹰飞到距离鸟巢十英尺[1]以内的地方。"

"蛇能爬那么高吗？"露丝问。

乔希得意地笑了笑，说："可以，像蛇一样的人就能！"

"什么意思？"丁丁问，"你觉得有人偷走了那些游隼？"

乔希点了点头。

"但是谁会做这样的事呢？"露丝问。

"我不知道。"乔希说，"但是我们会找出那个人的！"

1.英尺：英美制长度单位。1英尺=0.3048米。——编者

第三章

第二天早上，丁丁按响了露丝家的门铃。她穿着一套绿色的慢跑运动服来开门，甚至连她的运动鞋和束发带都是绿色的。

"你看起来像一丛灌木。"丁丁说。

露丝咧着嘴笑了笑，然后朝屋子里大喊："妈妈，我走了！"

她和丁丁一起前往林荫街接乔希。他们准备再去游隼的鸟巢那里寻找线索。

乔希住在农场路尽头的一所黄色的大房子

游隼的羽毛

里。房子后面有一座白色的谷仓。乔希正在对着钉在谷仓门上的铁环投篮。

他穿着迷彩衬衫和裤子。

"天哪!"丁丁说,"为什么你们不告诉我,你们都准备伪装成树!"

三个孩子顺着沿河路匆匆而去,然后沿着自行车道进入树林。就在他们快到那片空地的时候,乔希停了下来。一个穿着牛仔裤和法兰绒衬衫的男人正站在有游隼的那棵树下,抬头看着树枝。

孩子们面面相觑,然后走进空地。

那个男人转过身来。他有着卷曲的黑发,黝黑的脸庞,蓝色的眼睛。

"你们好。"男人说,"你们在这里干什么呢?"

"我们在远足。"乔希谨慎地回答道。

那个男人笑了笑。"等一下,你的声音好熟悉。你就是昨天打电话到我办公室说游隼失踪的那个人吗?"

乔希咧着嘴笑了笑。"是的,就是我。"乔希介绍道,"这两位是我的朋友,丁丁和露丝。"

A to Z 神秘案件

"很高兴认识你们。"男人说,"我叫库尔特。听着,小朋友们,我知道你们想帮忙,但是你们能做的最好的事就是离这里远一点。要是成年游隼看见或者闻见你们的气味,它们就不会回来了。"

"但是我们回来是为了寻找线索。"乔希说,"我觉得可能是有人带走了那些游隼。"

库尔特看起来很惊讶。"有人带走的?好吧,

我想也是有可能的。但是我不这么觉得。我已经看过这片区域,找不到一点人类的迹象或其他的线索。"

库尔特离开那棵树的时候,孩子们也跟着他离开了。"环境保护部感谢你们的来电。"库尔特说,"但是剩下的就交给我们吧。我相信我们很快就会解决这件事的。"

到了小路后,库尔特向右转过身。"再次谢谢你们!"他说。他朝孩子们挥了挥手,然后沿着小路慢跑起来。

孩子们沿着小路朝另一个方向走去。突然,乔希停了下来。"听!"他说。

"什么?"露丝问。

"我听见了些声音。"乔希在一丛杂草边俯身跪了下来。慢慢地,他用手指拨开了杂草。

一只棕色的小鸟蜷缩在杂草中。它的喙很锋利,一双黑眼睛闪闪发亮。

"是一只小游隼!"乔希说,"这肯定是鸟巢里的游隼!"

那只游隼正浑身发抖。它张开嘴,对着乔希

发出"咔咔、咔咔"的声音。它闪亮的眼睛一直盯着乔希的脸。

"这只可怜的小家伙看起来好像很害怕。"露丝说。

乔希脱下T恤,将它小心翼翼地盖在小鸟的身上。"如果它看不到我们,就不会那么害怕了。"乔希解释道。他将被T恤包着的小鸟抱在胸前。

"我们应该怎么安置它呢?"丁丁问。

"我们不能把它留在这里。"乔希说,"会有东西吃掉它的。"

"我们把它带到翁太太那里吧!"露丝说。

孩子们沿着小路匆匆走去。乔希抚摸着小鸟的羽毛,用轻柔的声音安抚它。

"嘿,这是什么?"乔希一边说着,一边轻轻地拉出游隼的一条腿。

游隼的腿上缠着一条细细的金属带子。

第四章

翁太太仔细检查着那条带子。"上面有字。"她告诉孩子们,"但是对我来说,字太小了,我认不出来。"

"那是什么?"乔希问。

"是一个名牌。"翁太太说,"就像你们给狗挂上项圈一样,有人觉得这只鸟是他的。"

乔希抱着那只游隼,游隼的部分身体还包在他的T恤里。它静静地坐着,看着眼前的人类。

"我在想它是不是饿了。"露丝说,"游隼吃什么呢?"

"游隼主要吃其他鸟类。"乔希说,"但是它们也会吃鱼和其他东西。"

"让我们找找有什么吃的吧!"翁太太说。她打开一个小冰箱,从里面拿出一些生汉堡,扯下一大块肉,放在游隼的嘴下。

"来啊,快吃了它。"乔希喃喃地说。

突然,游隼的头猛地向前伸去。它快速地咬了一大口,肉就不见了。

"好家伙,我觉得它是饿了!"露丝说,"吃这么快,我们应该叫它'闪电'!"

闪电开始发出响亮而刺耳的叫声。它一遍又一遍地尖叫着,直到翁太太又喂给它一块汉堡肉才停下来。喂了两次肉后,它就没再发出令人烦躁的声音,还闭上了眼睛。

"我们应该怎么安置它?"乔希问翁太太。

翁太太走到电话旁边。"首先,我们应该叫亨利医生来给它做个检查。"

孩子们听着翁太太向那位兽医说完关于闪电的事。她挂断电话后,说:"如果你们能把这只

游隼的羽毛

小鸟带去他的办公室,他就会给它检查一下。他就在东绿街。"

乔希再次用他的T恤包好闪电,孩子们便急匆匆地赶往亨利医生的办公室了。

乔希洗手的时候,亨利医生仔细检查了闪电。"你们在哪里发现这只小鸟的?"亨利医生问。

"就在树林里。"乔希一边说,一边穿上他的T恤。他向亨利医生解释了他们去看小游隼,却发现鸟巢里面是空的。

"嗯,这是一只小游隼,是的。"兽医说,"在这儿还挺罕见的。"

医生发现了闪电腿上的金属带子,把它剪断了。然后他轻轻地拨开这只游隼的翅膀,检查它身上是否有断骨。

"它看起来很健康,"医生说,"可能才刚学飞。但你们看这里,有人修剪了它翅膀上的羽毛!"

孩子们都聚了过来。

"看见了吗?"医生接着说,"游隼的翅膀通常是又长又尖的。这些羽毛被剪刀修剪成圆的了。"

就在这时,一个黑发的高个子女人走到桌子

前。"大家都在看什么呢?"她问。

"哦,你好呀,格蕾丝。"医生说,"孩子们,这是我的新助手,格蕾丝·洛克伍德。格蕾丝,这些孩子带来一只小游隼。"

那个女人直直地看了孩子们一眼。她眼神锐利,让丁丁想起了老鹰的眼睛。

她转过身,用手抚摸着小鸟的背部。突然,

闪电咬了她的手指一口。"哎哟!"她叫道。

亨利兽医咯咯地笑了起来:"最好还是戴上你的手套,格蕾丝。"

"我们应该怎么安置它呢?"乔希问。

"我会在这儿照看它几天。"医生说,"我们会确保它没事的。然后我们再决定怎么安置它。"

孩子们说了再见后,回到了主街。

"嗯,起码它在这儿是安全的。"乔希说,"我在想另外两只游隼去哪儿了。"

"在闪电逃跑之前,它们肯定在一起!"露丝说。

"我想知道的是,"丁丁说,"为什么会有人修剪闪电的翅膀。"

"要不我们去问问库尔特吧?"乔希说,"他知道很多关于游隼的事情。"

第五章

  消防站旁边有个小牌子，上面写着：环境保护部，请下楼。一个绿色的箭头指明了方向。到了楼下，孩子们来到一扇门前，门上写着"环境保护部"。

  办公室里空无一人，只有几张桌子和一堆靠墙放着的文件柜。文件柜上放着一只装在玻璃柜里的猫头鹰标本。

  就在这时，门开了。一位穿着T恤和棕褐色短裤的女士走了进来。"我能帮你们什么吗？"她

A to Z 神秘案件

问孩子们。

"我们来找库尔特。"乔希说。

"斯特莱克先生通常回家吃午餐,"她说,"要不然你们晚些时候再来?"

"这事挺重要的。"乔希说,"他住在绿地镇吗?我们可以走过去找他。"

女人指了指墙上的城镇地图。"他是新来的,但我想他现在应该在大桥路租了间小屋。你们知道那个地方在哪儿吗?"

"当然知道。"丁丁说,"他肯定住在河边,对吧?"

那个女人点了点头。"没错,只要找到他的棕色皮卡车就能找到他了。"

孩子们离开消防站,徒步向大桥路去了。绿地镇的这片区域只有几所房子。其中大多数房子周围都是树木和茂密的灌木丛。

"那肯定是了。"乔希说。他们站在一扇木栅栏前,旁边是一排松树。树木中间有一条砾石车道,通向一间小木屋。

"看,那儿有辆棕色卡车!"丁丁说。

当孩子们走进大门时,他们看见库尔特·斯特莱克坐在小木屋的小门廊上。他正在吃一块三明治。

库尔特从门廊上跳了下来,朝孩子们走去。

A to Z 神秘案件

"嘿,孩子们。"他说,"是什么事让你们到这儿来了?"

乔希和他说了他们在树林里发现了一只小游隼的事。

游隼的羽毛

"不仅如此。"露丝说,"有人在它的腿上绑了条带子,还修剪了它的翅膀!"

"真的吗?"库尔特说着,一副若有所思的样子,"看起来我欠你一声道歉,乔希。确实是有人带走了那些游隼。"

乔希害羞地笑了笑。

"为什么会有人修剪它的翅膀呢?"丁丁问。

"这个嘛,"库尔特说,"最有可能的原因就是有人在训练它做什么事。"

"比如说?"露丝问。

库尔特耸了耸肩。"可能是很多种不同的事。"

他们一边说话,库尔特一边陪着孩子们向大桥路走去。"那只游隼现在在哪儿?"他问。

"我们把它带去看兽医了。"乔希说,"亨利医生说他会照看好它的。"

库尔特点了点头。"谢谢你们来告知我。我一定会和亨利医生联系的。"

孩子们说了再见后,又回到主街。

"我希望他能抓住那个带走游隼的人。"露丝说,"剪掉小鸟的羽毛真是太卑鄙了!"

乔希点了点头。"是啊,但是至少这不会疼。我想就像你剪掉脚指甲一样吧。"

他们走过埃莉餐馆。格蕾丝·洛克伍德正坐在窗户旁边,一边看书一边吃着午餐。当她注意到孩子们在看着她时,她也隔着玻璃回望孩

子们。

　　她面无表情，但她的眼神使孩子们赶紧走开了。

　　"她看起来好像很不安。"露丝说。

　　"也许她只是不喜欢孩子们在她吃东西的时候盯着她看。"丁丁说。

　　"你们看到她在读什么书了吗？"乔希问。

　　"某本杂志吧。"丁丁说。

"不是普通的杂志。"乔希一边说，一边看向丁丁和露丝，"我认得那个封面，那本杂志是《今日游隼》。"

第六章

"我觉得乔希生病了。"露丝小声对丁丁说。

"我没生病。"乔希说着,又咬了一口他的金枪鱼三明治。

孩子们正在丁丁家的野餐桌上吃午餐。

"那你为什么这么安静?"露丝问,"你今天一整天都没有呛我!"

乔希吃着他的三明治。"一会儿我再呛你,"他说,"现在我正在想那些失踪的游隼的事。"他看向他的朋友们。"我觉得是格蕾丝·洛克伍德带走了它们。"他补充道。

"格蕾丝·洛克伍德!"丁丁说,"为什么你会觉得是她?"

"你们也看到她看的那本杂志了,"乔希说,"那本杂志是关于游隼的。"

露丝点了点头。"她在亨利医生那里也表现得有点奇怪。"

"是啊,别忘了她在埃莉餐馆看我们的眼神,"乔希说,"她可是在盯着我呢。"

"盯着你?"丁丁说,"乔希,她盯着我们是因为我们在盯着她!"

乔希偷偷地拿了一根露丝的胡萝卜条。"我们回兽医诊所再和她聊聊吧。"他说,"也许她会说一些线索!"

丁丁起身准备出发。"好吧,但是我觉得你想错了,乔希。因为格蕾丝·洛克伍德看关于游隼的杂志并不意味着她会去掏鸟窝。"

兽医诊所里,孩子们透过窗户凝视着格蕾丝·洛克伍德。

"快看！"乔希小声说，"她正戴着长皮手套！捕猎游隼的人就会戴那样的手套！"

"消防员也会戴这样的手套。"丁丁说。

他们走了进去。格蕾丝·洛克伍德正要把一只乌鸦放到桌子上。乌鸦的腿上和脖子周围都缠着塑料。

她抬头看了看。"有什么事吗？"她问。

"嗯，我们来看看闪电怎么样了。"露丝说，"这只乌鸦怎么了？"

格蕾丝摇了摇头。"身上缠着六块塑料！"

孩子们看着格蕾丝小心翼翼地用剪刀剪开塑料。

乌鸦啄了好几次她的手套。丁丁看着浑身发抖。它的喙看起来十分尖锐！

乌鸦身上的塑料被解开后，格蕾丝向大楼的后门走去。"你们可以帮我开一下门吗？"她说。

丁丁打开门后，扶着门站在旁边。格蕾丝带着乌鸦穿过一个满是笼子和围栏的小院子。

她把那只黑色的乌鸦抛向空中。"不要再被塑料缠到了！"她大声说道。那只乌鸦随后便消

A to Z 神秘案件

失在树林中。

丁丁环顾四周，看了看这个小院子。它有一个篮球场那么大，四周围起了高高的木栅栏，还有一扇门。

丁丁看到一个笼子里有一只熟睡的臭鼬。其他笼子里还关着浣熊和兔子。他看到了几条蛇，还有一群鸟。他还看到了一只狐狸宝宝！

"我一直以为兽医只照看猫猫狗狗呢。"乔希说。

"有些兽医是那样的。"格蕾丝说，"我刚好喜欢野生动物。"

乔希看着丁丁和露丝，动了动眉毛。

"闪电在哪里？"乔希一边问，一边看了看周围的几个笼子。

"我把它放在这儿了。"她一边说着，一边走向院子的一个角落，"医生喜欢将新来的动物与其他动物分开。"

格蕾丝在一个盖着小毛毯的笼子前停了下来。"它可能正在睡觉。"她说。

她拿开毛毯。笼子的底部铺着稻草，里面是

游隼的羽毛

一段中空的原木。

"它就躲在里面。"格蕾丝说。她轻轻地拍了拍笼子的侧面。

"真奇怪。"她一边说着,一边打开笼子的门。她摇了摇那根木头,往里面看了看。

"怎么了?"露丝问。

"它不见了。"格蕾丝说。

第七章

"什么?!"乔希朝笼子里看了看,"闪电怎么会不见了?"

"我不知道。"格蕾丝说,"我还是赶紧去通知医生吧。"

她匆忙走向办公室。"这有点可疑。"露丝说,"闪电怎么会凭空消失呢?"

"肯定是又有人把它偷走了!"乔希说。

亨利医生和格蕾丝快步穿过院子。亨利医生边走边脱他的外科手术手套。

"午餐前它还在笼子里的。"格蕾丝说。

亨利医生弯下腰,朝笼子里看了看。"真令人难以置信。"他嘀咕着,"大门上锁了吗?"

格蕾丝点了点头。"我觉得应该是上了的。我再去检查一下。"她跑向院子里的一个角落,"锁被人撬开了!"

医生和孩子们都匆忙过去看了看。院子里厚厚的木门是关着的,但是锁已经被人撬开了。木头和金属碎片散落在地上。

亨利医生捡起地上的金属碎片。"肯定是有人想进入这里。"他说,"这锁是市场上质量最好的锁!"

丁丁仔细检查了一下大门。"我在想木门上会不会有指纹。"他说。

"可能有。"医生说。

"我们要不要叫法伦警官?"丁丁问。

"这个建议极好。"亨利医生说着,朝办公室走去。

"我还是先把锁修好吧。"格蕾丝说道。她连"再见"都没说就匆匆走开了。

A to Z 神秘案件

孩子们也离开了。他们经过清水塘，回到主街。"我敢打赌，是格蕾丝撬开了那把锁，让它看起来像是有人破门而入。"乔希说。

丁丁摇了摇头。"格蕾丝是帮助动物的，乔希。"

"小鸟会有记忆吗？"露丝突然问道。

"为什么这么问？"丁丁问。

"嗯，还记得我们第一次带闪电来亨利医生办公室的时候吗？它啄了格蕾丝的手。"

"是的，所以？"

露丝停下脚步，看着丁丁和乔希。"嗯，如果格蕾丝爬上树带走了那些游隼，也许闪电还记得她。也许就是因为这样，它才啄她的！"

"你们太急于下结论了。"丁丁说。他在主街按了下行人过街按钮[1]。

"我想我们需要多了解一点游隼。"他说。

"丁丁说得没错。"露丝对乔希说，"如果我们对它们了解得更多，也许我们就能弄清楚为什

1.行人过街按钮：控制信号，使机动车道绿灯变为红灯，人行横道红灯变为绿灯。主要安装在过街需求不均衡、车流量又较大的丁字路口或路段，方便行人通过。——编者

么会有人带走它们了。"

"我们为什么不去图书馆呢?"丁丁穿过主街时建议。

"好。"乔希说,"但是格蕾丝·洛克伍德依然排在我的嫌疑人名单榜首!"

"还有谁在你的嫌疑人名单中?"露丝问。

乔希慢跑着穿过街道。"没有了!"

第八章

孩子们走进图书馆时,迈克尔罗伊太太正在给一本书粘封面。

"嘿,孩子们。"她说,"有人太喜欢这本书了,以至于他们把封面都撕掉了!"

她粘好封面,然后在上面压上一本厚厚的书,使它保持平整。"好了,"她一边说,一边擦掉手指上的胶水,"那么我今天怎样可以帮到你们呢?"

"我们想找一些关于游隼的信息。"乔希告

游隼的羽毛

诉她。

迈克尔罗伊太太指了指电脑桌。"你们知道怎么用电脑检索吗?"她问。

"当然,我们在学校经常用电脑。"露丝说,"快来,朋友们!"

丁丁坐在电脑面前,乔希和露丝看向电脑。丁丁输入"FALCONS",然后按下回车键。

几秒钟后,屏幕上出现一长串书名。

"天哪,这肯定有五十本书是关于猎鹰的。"乔希说。

"试试输入'PEREGRINE'。[1]"露丝说。丁丁输入新单词后,列表缩短了不少——图书馆有四本关于游隼的书。

丁丁把那张较短的单子打印出来,拿给迈克尔罗伊太太。

"这些书在儿童阅读室。"迈克尔罗伊太太一边说,一边在其中两本书的书名旁边打钩。

1.游隼的英文是 peregrine falcon,所以丁丁输入"FALCONS"检索出来的书名较多后,露丝建议丁丁输入"PEREGRINE"。——编者

53

孩子们找到了两本书中的一本，书名是《游隼：皇家猛禽》。他们一起挤在一条长凳上，迅速翻着这本书。

这本书讲述了游隼是如何因为杀虫剂而近乎灭绝的。

他们又翻了几页，直到看到"神奇的游隼知识"这章才停下来。

"游隼很容易训练。"乔希大声地读了出来。

"还有，快看，上面说游隼从一而终。"露丝补充道。

"快看第七点。"丁丁一边说，一边将手指向

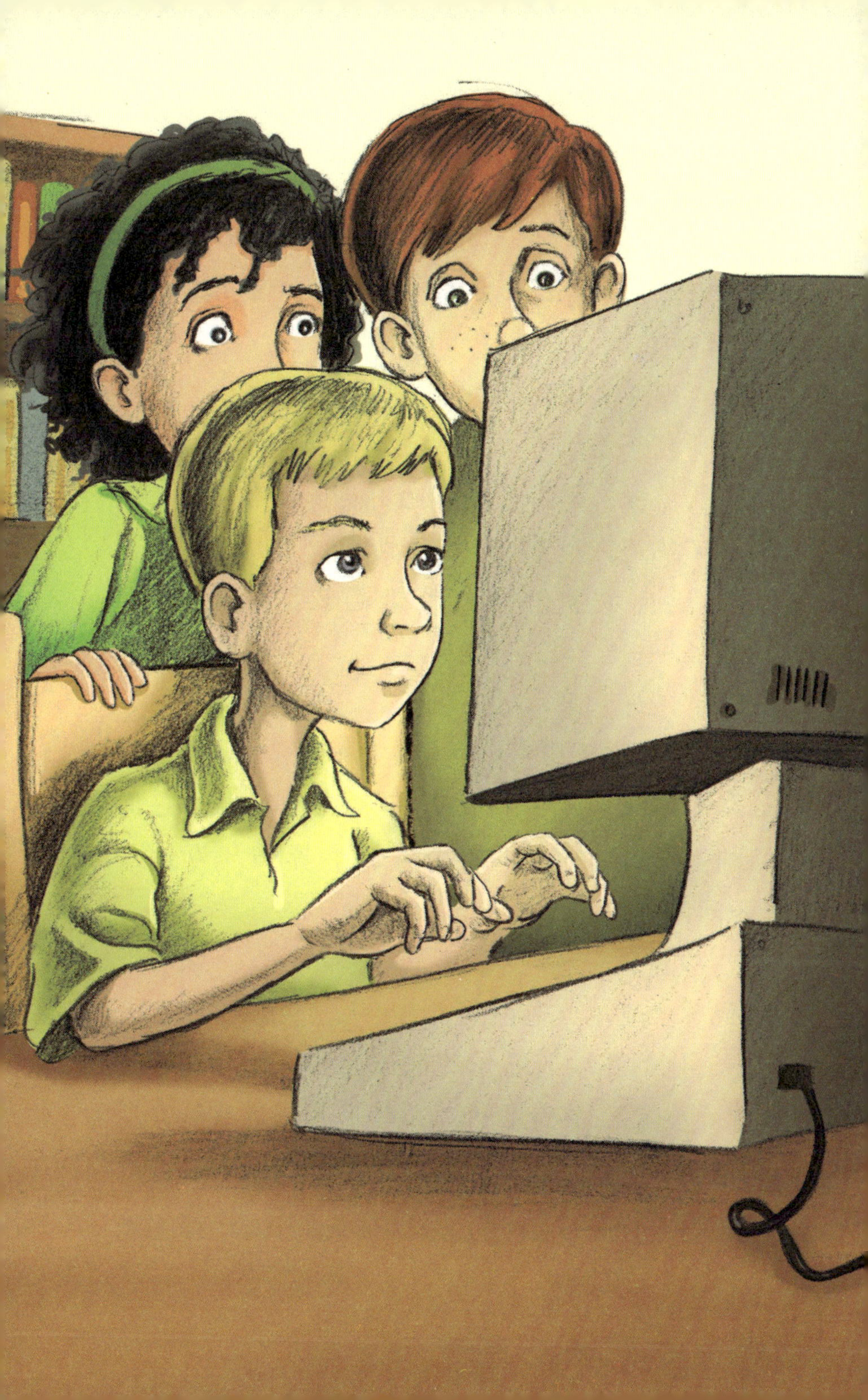

那页的下部移动,"游隼是自然界速度最快的猎手之一。在追逐鸟类时,游隼的时速可达每小时二百英里[1]!"

"那可比猎豹还快!"乔希说。

"我爸爸的车每小时也只能开一百英里。"丁丁说,"哇,那游隼比赛岂不是很好看。"

"就是这个!"露丝大喊道。

迈克尔罗伊太太用铅笔敲了敲桌子,说:"露丝——"

"不好意思。"露丝说。

孩子们还了书,急忙跑了出去。

"我敢打赌,一定是有人在偷游隼让它们比赛!"露丝说,"人类会赛狗和赛马,为什么不会赛游隼呢?"

"我们将这些事告诉库尔特吧。"乔希说,"他甚至还不知道闪电又被人偷走了。"

他们在埃莉餐馆的电话亭打电话给环境保护部办公室。乔希告诉库尔特有人闯进兽医诊所偷

1.英里:英美制长度单位。1英里=1.6093千米。——编者

游隼的羽毛

走了闪电,然后他又将他们在图书馆了解到的信息告诉了他。

过了一会儿,乔希挂断了电话。"他马上就过来。"

"真的吗?"丁丁说。

"是的,"乔希说,"他来之前我可以先吃一个开心果甜筒!"

露丝买了她常点的草莓甜筒。丁丁买了他最喜欢的黄油脆饼甜筒。孩子们坐在一个隔间里,各自吃着自己的甜筒。

"你们知道的,我一直在想,"露丝一边舔着甜筒,一边说,"除了我们,还有谁知道闪电在兽医诊所?"

丁丁和乔希看着她。"嗯,翁太太知道。"丁丁说。

"当然,她是不会破门进去偷走闪电的!"乔希说。

"亨利医生也知道,但我觉得不会是他。"丁丁说。

露丝瞥了她的朋友们一眼。"还有谁?"

"格蕾丝·洛克伍德!"乔希说。

"别忘了,库尔特也知道。"丁丁说,"我们告诉过他,闪电在亨利医生那儿。"

乔希摇了摇头。"库尔特的工作就是保护野生动物。"

就在这时,库尔特·斯特莱克走进餐馆。他点了一杯咖啡,然后溜进隔间。"所以你们一直在做侦探工作,嗯?"他问。

"有人从兽医诊所将闪电偷了出来!"露丝对库尔特说。

"我知道。"库尔特说,"乔希在电话里告诉我了。但是谁是闪电?"

她咧嘴笑了笑。"就是那只游隼!我们叫它闪电,因为它吃东西可快了。"

"那赛游隼是怎么回事?"库尔特问这话的时候,看着乔希。

"嗯,我们了解到游隼每小时可以飞二百英里!"乔希说,"所以我们觉得可能会有人训练它们来比赛。"

库尔特喝了一口咖啡。"赛游隼?嗯,这想

法挺有趣的。"

"赛游隼可以赚钱吗?"丁丁问库尔特,"就像赛马赚钱那样?"

库尔特缓缓点了点头。"是的,我想可以的。"

他喝完了他的咖啡。"这样吧,我去找找我的几个熟人,谈谈你们的想法。但与此同时,这事我们要保密,好吗?"

"你真的觉得你能找出是谁带走了这些游隼吗?"露丝说。

库尔特一骨碌就从座位上起来了。"你们可以放心。"他说。

第九章

孩子们走出埃莉餐馆,看见法伦警官就站在拐角处。

"嘿,孩子们,"他说,"天气这么好,你们在这里干什么呢?"

"你好,法伦警官,"丁丁说,"亨利医生和你说有人闯进兽医诊所的事了吗?"

法伦警官按下交通灯杆上的行人过街按钮。他拿着一个黑色的小箱子。"我正带着我的指纹工具包朝那里赶呢。"他说,"亨利医生和我说有只游隼不见了。但你们这些孩子是怎么参与到这些事当中的？"

乔希和法伦警官说了自己发现游隼鸟巢的经过。

"我们昨天去看的时候，游隼都不见了。"露丝说。

"而且我们觉得，我们知道这事是谁干的！"乔希说。

乔希和露丝两人你一言，我一语，解释了他们如何认定格蕾丝·洛克伍德是偷走游隼并训练它们比赛的人。

"哦，我不觉得是她。"丁丁说。

法伦警官缓缓地点了点头。"听我说。"他说，"我们到那儿时，只要观察和倾听就好了。"他微笑着说，"也许我们会发现一些新东西。"

法伦警官和孩子们走进亨利医生的外部办公室。透过窗户，他们看见亨利医生和格蕾丝正在给一只狗的腿打石膏。

"做兽医也不错。"乔希说，"可以整天都和动物一起玩。"

"那不是玩,乔希,那是份辛苦的工作。"法伦警官说,"有的兽医半夜都会被叫出去!而且,我还以为你想成为一名鸟类艺术家呢。"

乔希咧嘴笑了笑。"我不能兼顾吗?"他说。

亨利医生走了出来,一边走还一边擦着手指上的石膏泥。"谢谢你过来。"他对法伦警官说,"快来,我带你们看看我的锁还剩下什么。"

孩子们看着格蕾丝将狗带离桌子,放进一个笼子里,然后给了它一块狗吃的曲奇饼干。

"你们误会格蕾丝了。"丁丁小声地说,"她真的很喜欢动物。"

"很多坏人也喜欢动物。"乔希提醒丁丁。

露丝用手肘推了推他们。"快走吧,我们去看法伦警官采指纹。"

问题是,木门上面没有任何指纹。法伦警官在上面撒了一层灰,但是没有出现指纹。"好吧,我猜他擦了门或者戴了手套。"法伦警官说。

"或者是'她'戴了手套。"乔希喃喃地说。

丁丁记起了一些事。"翁太太说,小游隼腿上的带子上有一些小小的字。"他对亨利医生说,

"你看了吗?"

"我当然看了,丁丁。过来这边,我带你们去看看。"

法伦警官和孩子们走进办公室。格蕾丝·洛克伍德正在桌子旁填写一些文件。乔希一直盯着她,直到丁丁轻轻推了他一下。

"把那条带子递给我,可以吗,格蕾丝?"亨利医生问。

格蕾丝点了点头,将带子递给了亨利医生。医生从桌子上拿起一个放大镜,把它和带子一起递给丁丁。"告诉我你看到了什么,小伙子。"

丁丁透过放大镜,仔细分辨着带子上的字。"我看到了一些字母和数字。"他说。

"你能读出来吗?"

"GLKS 6-17。"丁丁读了出来。读完,他抬起头,问:"这是什么意思?"

亨利医生拿起带子和放大镜。

"这些字母我还不知道是什么意思,但是这些数字很可能是日期。"他说,"如果我没说错的话,这些数字代表着闪电生于6/17,也就是6月

17日。"

"那这些字母会不会是带走闪电的人的姓名缩写?"乔希问。

"这个思路很好。"亨利医生说,"这些字母如果是姓名缩写的话,那是谁的姓名缩写呢?"

"没有留下任何指纹。"法伦警官说,"我要说我们的这个贼,像小鸟一样飞走了!"

丁丁偷偷地看了一眼格蕾丝。她的白色夹克外面挂着她的名牌。也许带子上的"GL"代表

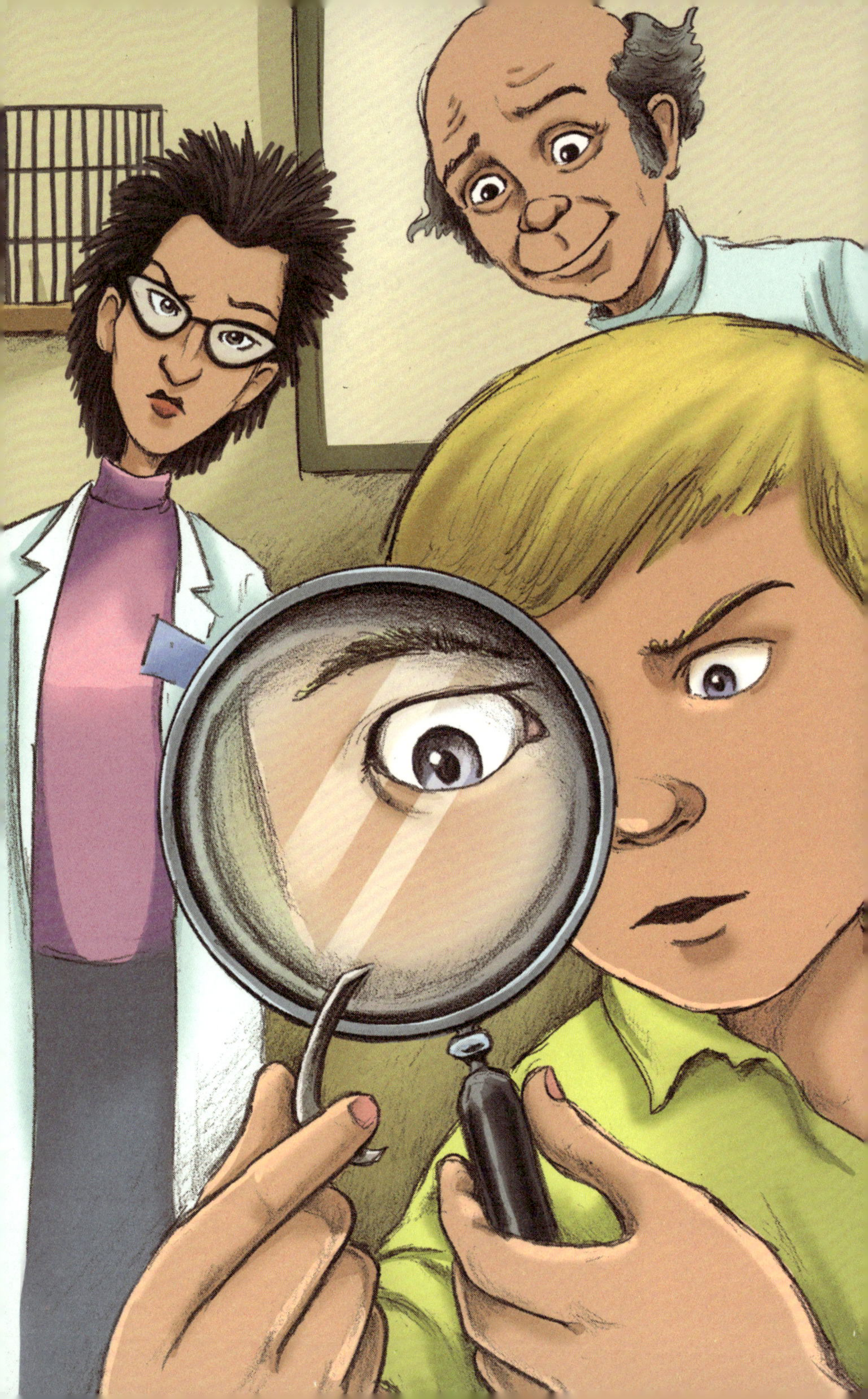

的就是格蕾丝·洛克伍德![1]

丁丁倒吸了一口气。难道乔希说得没错?格蕾丝·洛克伍德到底有没有带走游隼?

---

1. 格蕾丝·洛克伍德的英文为 Grace Lockwood,缩写恰好是"GL"。——编者

第十章

孩子们陪着法伦警官回到了西绿街的警察局。
"你会去逮捕她吗?"乔希问。
"逮捕谁,乔希?"
"格蕾丝·洛克伍德!"乔希说。
法伦警官笑了笑,摇了摇头。"我们没有任何证据证明她做了错事。"
丁丁决定对带子上的字母"GL"只字不提。乔希已经想把格蕾丝·洛克伍德送进监狱了!
"不要担心,乔希。"法伦警官接着说,"不管是谁做的，我相信我们都会抓到那个人。"

孩子们看着他走进警察局。"走吧。"丁丁说，"我们去动物园玩一会儿吧。"

"丁丁，你不关心那些游隼了吗？"乔希问。

"我当然关心了。但你也听到了法伦警官说的话，"丁丁一边说，一边穿过西绿街，"我们没有任何证据证明是格蕾丝·洛克伍德做的。"

乔希踢了一块石头。"你们相信我，她真的有些古怪！"

丁丁笑了。"乔希，你觉得她有古怪是因为她抓到你盯着她的芝士汉堡了！"

孩子们绕过图书馆，进入了动物园。骆驼和小鹿啃食着孩子们手上的饲料。一只大鹅带着六只小鹅摇摇摆摆地走着。笼子里有几只动物，但大多是零零散散的。

几个青少年在走来走去地卖动物食品。他们穿着深绿色的短裤和衬衫，衬衫上印着大大的圆形徽章。徽章上写着"GLPZ"，意思是绿地镇动物园。[1]

"等一下,朋友们,"露丝说,"我想去喂小鹿。"

丁丁和乔希看着她急匆匆地跑向其中一个少年。

"好吧,我还是觉得那个人是格蕾丝·洛克伍德。"乔希坚持他的想法,"我们应该告诉库尔特关于她的事。"

"告诉他什么事,她瞪了你一眼吗?"丁丁问。

"首先,我要告诉他带子上有一些单词的首字母缩写。"乔希说,"他可能知道那是什么意思。"

露丝回来时手上拿着一小袋饲料。"你们想来一些吗?"她问丁丁和乔希。

"最好还是不要给乔希。"丁丁说,"他可能会吃了它们!"

"哈哈。"乔希一边笑,一边从露丝的包里拿出几粒饲料。

他们喂完骆驼和小鹿后,离开了动物园。

乔希从香格里拉酒店大厅给库尔特·斯特莱

---

1. 绿地镇动物园的全称是 Green Lawn Petting Zoo。——译者

A to Z 神秘案件

克的办公室打了电话。

他挂了电话,说:"没人接。"

"那现在怎么办?"露丝问。

"我们再去他的小木屋找找看吧。"乔希说,"如果他不在那儿,我们可以留张字条。"

"留字条说什么呢?"丁丁问。

乔希从口袋里掏出一支铅笔,然后从酒店职员林克莱特先生那里拿来一张纸,在上面写了起来。

"就说这个。"他说完,将字条拿给丁丁和露丝看。

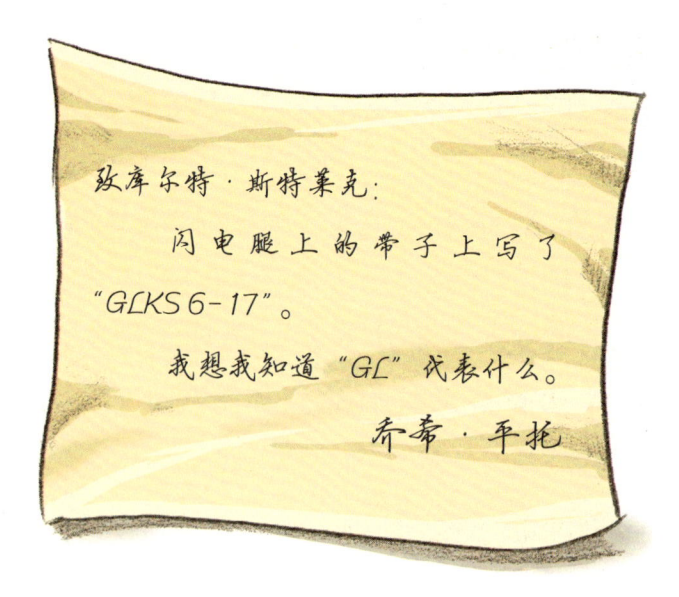

致库尔特·斯特莱克:

闪电腿上的带子上写了"GLKS 6-17"。

我想我知道"GL"代表什么。

乔希·平托

丁丁盯着乔希，问："你认为'GL'代表什么？"

乔希咧嘴笑了笑。"格蕾丝·洛克伍德！"

"那'KS'呢？"露丝问。

乔希耸了耸肩。"那就要问库尔特了。快走吧！"

孩子们沿着沿河路徒步前往大桥路。走到一半时，露丝突然停了下来。

"怎么了？"丁丁问。

她抬头直直地望着天空。"我在想一些东西。是我在环境保护部办公室看到的，但是我记不起是什么了！"

"也许是那个猫头鹰标本吧。"乔希说着，向露丝瞪了一个猫头鹰般大的眼睛。

"不，我想是我在桌子上看到的某些东西。"她在尘土飞扬的路上跺着脚，"我怎么就记不起来了呢？"

几分钟后，他们到达了库尔特的小木屋。乔希走上前，敲了敲门。

没人回应。

"我猜他不在家。"丁丁说。

"也许他在后院。"乔希说,"我们去那儿看看吧。"

后院除了一堆柴火,什么也没有。

露丝指着一条通往树林的土路。"也许他昨天就是从这儿到树林里的。"她说。

突然,他们听到一阵低沉的哨声。

"那是什么声音?"乔希问。

"也许只是有人在叫他的狗吧。"丁丁说,"快走吧,离开这里。我们这是非法入侵他人住宅。"

哨声再次响起。乔希沿着小路跑过去。"那是游隼的叫声!"他说。

丁丁和露丝跟在乔希后面。他们发现乔希在一个小棚子前停了下来。小棚子一边的窗扇被撑开了。

"听。"乔希小声地说。

孩子们听见小棚子里传来啾啾声和更多的口哨声。

"里面有游隼!"乔希说着,跑到旁边,开始

游隼的羽毛

用力拉门上的一把厚厚的挂锁。

"这蠢玩意儿上锁了!"乔希说。

露丝回到窗户旁边。"扶我一把,朋友们。"

丁丁和乔希手臂交叉。露丝爬了上去,将自己撑了起来。"里面大概有十个笼子,每个笼子都装着游隼!"她说。

乔希和丁丁把她放了下来。"我要进去。"乔希说。

"我们和你一起去!"露丝说。

几码[1]外的杂草丛里,有一个木桶。孩子们把它滚过来,放在窗下。

站在木桶上,乔希爬过了窗口。

露丝是第二个爬过去的人。接着是丁丁。

小棚子里面又冷又暗。借着窗户透出的微光,丁丁数了数,笼子里至少有十几只游隼。

小鸟们扇着翅膀,发出低沉的哨声。它们黑黑的眼睛注视着孩子们的一举一动。

突然,从窗外透过来的光被遮住了。库尔

---

1. 英美制长度单位,1 码 =0.9144 米。——编者

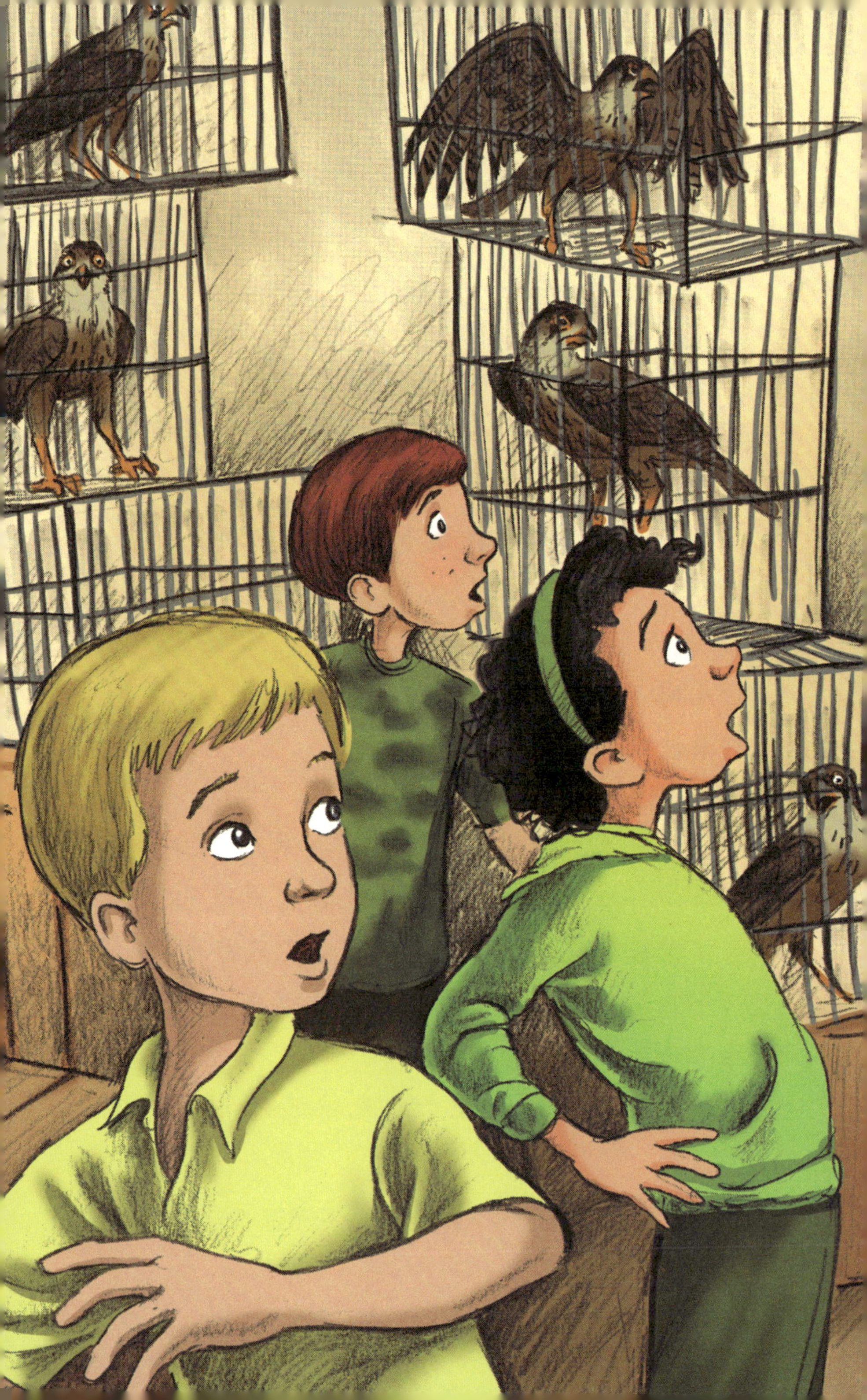

特·斯特莱克正瞪着他们！

"你们就不能只管好自己的事吗？！"他说，"一定要打探到底是吧？"

然后他的脸就从窗口消失了。过了一会儿，窗户砰的一下被关上了。

第十一章

丁丁盯着刚刚透着光的地方。他能感觉到露丝和乔希走近了。

"如果他不让我们出去怎么办？"露丝问。

"我们试试能不能打开那扇窗户吧。"丁丁说。

丁丁和乔希把露丝抬到窗户前。她用力将窗户往外推。"不行。"她说，"他肯定给窗户上了锁。"

他们试着推门，但门也被锁住了。

"我们该怎么办了，朋友们？"乔希问，"没有人知道我们在这儿!"

丁丁在昏暗的棚子里走来走去,摸着墙壁寻找出口。在一个角落里,他被一些耙子和铲子绊倒了。

"朋友们,快看!"露丝突然说。

"看什么?"乔希问。

"快看地面,我脚边的地面。"她说。

丁丁往下看,看见一个白色的圆点。

"是阳光!"乔希说。

他们一起抬头往上看。棚顶有一个小小的洞。

丁丁跑到角落那里抓起一把铲子。"也许我们可以从那个洞出去!"他说。

乔希拿了一把耙子。他们一起尝试着戳开那个小洞。

"我够不到!"乔希说。

"有些笼子是空的,"露丝说,"也许你们可以站在笼子上面!"

乔希和丁丁一起拖了四个笼子过去,搭建起一个平台。站在上面,他们发现自己很容易就能够到天花板。

他们使劲戳那个洞。几分钟后,洞被戳成了垒球大小。大块的木头、瓦片和沥青纸落在他们的头上和肩膀上。

丁丁停下来擦了擦眼睛。

"我的胳膊疼死了。"乔希一边说,一边坐在笼子上休息。

"起码现在我们看东西更清楚了。"露丝说道。她四处走了走,看了看笼子里的游隼。

"这些笼子都有标签。"她说,"前两个首字母不一样,但是后两个都是'KS'。"

"朋友们,我找到闪电了。"丁丁说。

他正看着一个笼子,笼子里关着三只小游隼。笼子门上贴的标签上写着"GLKS 6-17"。

"噢,我的天哪!"露丝大喊道,"我想起来我忘记的是什么了!"

"是什么?"丁丁问。

"我们去库尔特办公室的时候,我看见他的桌子上有个名牌。"她说,"他名字的首字母是'K'而不是'C'!"

"我不明白你的意思。"乔希说。

游隼的羽毛

"我明白。"丁丁说,"闪电腿上的带子上写的'KS'代表的是库尔特·斯特莱克。对吧,露丝?"

"对的!而且我相信'GL'代表的是绿地镇!"她说。

"我现在明白你的意思了。"乔希说,"他在带子上写的是他发现游隼的地方和他姓名的首字母。"

"我们必须将这件事告诉法伦警官。"露丝说。

"首先我们要离开这里!"乔希抓起耙子,又爬上那堆笼子。

丁丁和乔希一起猛击棚顶,棚顶的洞被戳得更大了。阳光倾洒在他们又湿又脏的脸上。

最终,戳出的大洞足够他们爬出去了。

"再多堆些笼子!"露丝说。

又堆了两个笼子后,孩子们能够爬上棚顶了。

他们坐了一会儿,呼吸着清新的空气,感受着阳光照在脸上的感觉。

"一直都是他在捣鬼。"乔希说道,语气里满是失落。

"最起码我们找到了这些游隼。"丁丁说。

A to Z 神秘案件

乔希走到棚顶的边缘,往下看了看。"木桶还在那里。"他说,"快来,我们可以爬下去。"

孩子们一落地,就朝主街和警察局跑去。

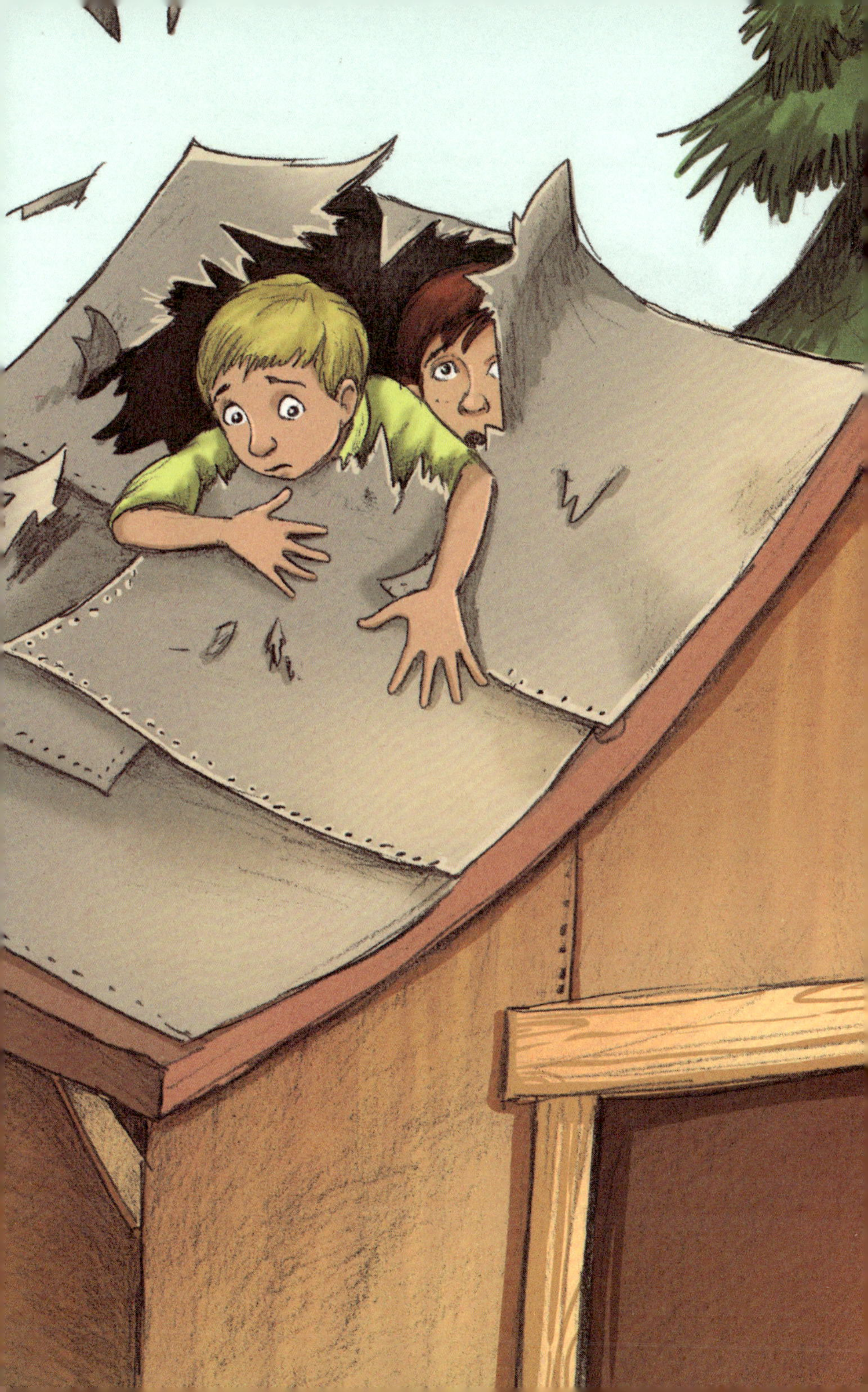

第十二章

一小时后,事情都结束了。亨利医生、格蕾丝·洛克伍德、法伦警官和孩子们坐在埃莉餐馆的一个隔间里。

"库尔特·斯特莱克在马萨诸塞州被抓住了。"法伦警官说,"他现在在斯普林菲尔德的监狱里坐牢,等着被运回这里。"

"所以是他从那个鸟巢里带走了游隼?"乔希问。

"不仅是那个鸟巢。"格蕾丝·洛克伍德说,

"据我们所知,他还去过另外三个州的鸟巢里抓游隼。"

亨利医生笑了笑。"我想我们还欠你们一个解释。"他说,"格蕾丝不是兽医,她是环境保护部的一个卧底。她被派到绿地镇只为一件事:密切监察我们的游隼数量。"

乔希看着格蕾丝。"我就知道你有点古怪!"

每个人都笑了起来。"格蕾丝知道鸟巢的事,"法伦警官告诉乔希,"她也知道你经常带着你的双筒望远镜去鸟巢那里。"

"我发现你在观察游隼。"格蕾丝说,"一开始我还以为是你带走了它们。"

"你觉得是乔希带走了游隼?"丁丁说,"乔希觉得是你!"

"我知道。"格蕾丝一边说,一边朝乔希笑了笑,"你一直在用奇怪的眼神看我!"

"你怀疑过库尔特·斯特莱克吗?"露丝问。

格蕾丝摇了摇头。"一点也没有。我们还要多谢你们发现了这一点。"

"那他偷游隼干什么呢?"丁丁问。

"至于那个,你们猜对了。"亨利医生说,"斯特莱克有个小生意。他带走这些小游隼,就是为了训练它们去比赛。"

"这些游隼以后会怎么样呢?"丁丁问。

"我们会将它们放生。"格蕾丝说,"但是它们与人类接触太多了,可能无法在野外生存。不过不用担心,有很多很好的动物园,可以让动物们幸福、安全地生活下去。"

"也许闪电可以住在绿地镇的动物园里!"乔希说。

"这个主意不错!"亨利医生说,"我会和他们谈谈收养闪电家三只游隼的事。"

"至于库尔特·斯特莱克,他将在监狱里待上一段时间。"法伦警官说,"毫无疑问,他会供出几个他的同伙,而那些同伙也会和他一起坐牢。"

埃莉端着一个大托盘走了过来。"免费冰激凌!"她说,"我为各位准备了香草——"

"但是我一直吃的是开心果味的!"乔希说。

"我还没说完呢,乔希。"埃莉说。

"你得原谅乔希。"露丝说,"他一饿就会脾

气暴躁。"

"而且他很容易饿!"丁丁说。

"就像我刚才说的,"埃莉继续说,"我为各位准备了香草冰激凌,但为乔希·平托,这个拯救了游隼的男孩,准备了不一样的东西!"

她在乔希面前放了一大盘开心果味冰激凌。"我希望你把这些都吃掉。"她笑着说。

"这倒不用担心,乔希,"丁丁说,"那些冰激凌会以闪电般的速度消失的!"

A to Z Mysteries®

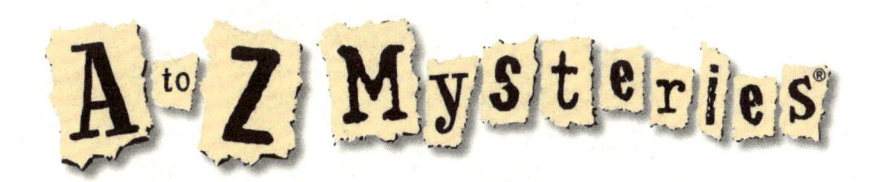

The Falcon's Feathers

by Ron Roy

illustrated by
John Steven Gurney

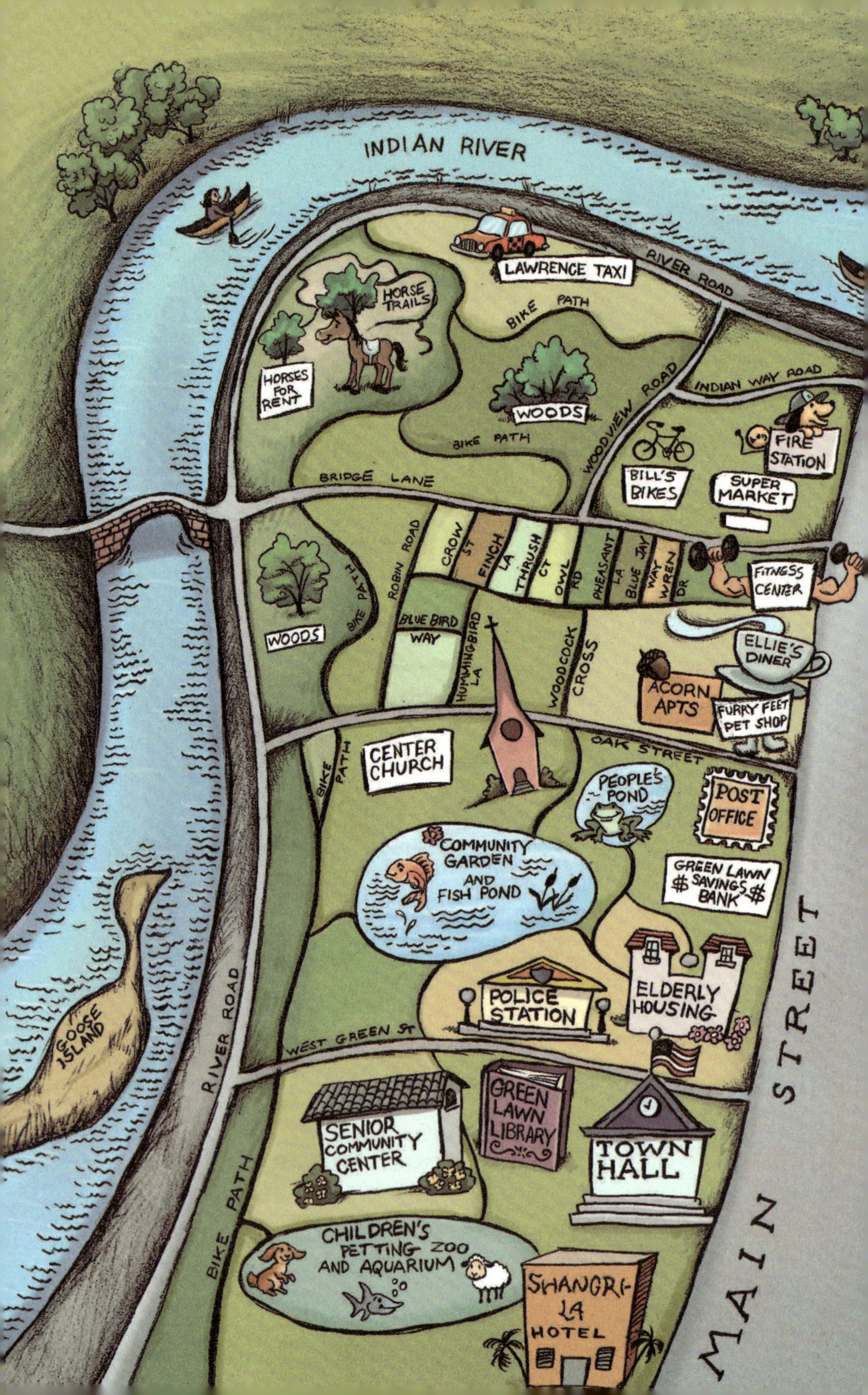
INDIAN RIVER
LAWRENCE TAXI
RIVER ROAD
HORSE TRAILS
HORSES FOR RENT
BIKE PATH
WOODS
BIKE PATH
WOODVIEW ROAD
INDIAN WAY ROAD
FIRE STATION
BILL'S BIKES
SUPER MARKET
BRIDGE LANE
ROBIN ROAD
CROW ST
FINCH LA
THRUSH CT
OWL RD
PHEASANT LA
BLUE JAY WAY
WREN DR
FITNESS CENTER
WOODS
BIKE PATH
BLUE BIRD WAY
HUMMINGBIRD LA
WOODCOCK CROSS
ELLIE'S DINER
ACORN APTS
FURRY FEET PET SHOP
OAK STREET
BIKE PATH
CENTER CHURCH
PEOPLE'S POND
POST OFFICE
COMMUNITY GARDEN AND FISH POND
GREEN LAWN $ SAVINGS $ BANK
GOOSE ISLAND
RIVER ROAD
POLICE STATION
ELDERLY HOUSING
WEST GREEN ST
MAIN STREET
SENIOR COMMUNITY CENTER
GREEN LAWN LIBRARY
TOWN HALL
BIKE PATH
CHILDREN'S PETTING ZOO AND AQUARIUM
SHANGRI-LA HOTEL

WELCOME TO
GREEN LAWN
HOME OF THE
A to Z Mysteries
N
W
E
S
RIVER ROAD
BOAT LAUNCH
SQUAW ISLAND
BOAT RENTAL
RON'S BAIT
DUCK WALK WAY
GREEN LAWN MIDDLE SCHOOL
FARM LANE
JOSH
EAGLE LANE
GREEN LAWN ELEMENTARY SCHOOL
DINK
RUTH ROSE
TREE TOP CIRCLE
MEADOW ROAD
FOX LANE
QUAIL RUN ROAD
SILVER CIRCLE
WOODY STREET
BAND SHELL
ROSE GARDEN
PLEASANT STREET
THISTLE COURT
WILDFLOWER WAY
ROSE STREET
CENTER PARK
SWAN POND
GREEN LAWN HIGH SCHOOL
PLAYING FIELDS
GYM + POOL
BOXWOOD LANE
HOWARD'S BARBER-SHOP
BOOK NOOK
CRYSTAL POND
GAS STATION
MYSTIC GREENHOUSE
DOG KENNEL + VETERINARIAN
RIVER ROAD
EAST GREEN STREET
TOWN TENNIS COURTS
TOWN SWIMMING POOL
KIDDIE POOL
TOWN BASEBALL FIELD
TO THE BLUE HILLS

Chapter 1

Dink stepped on a branch. It broke with a loud snap.

"Geez, Dink, you sound like an elephant!" Josh said. "We have to be quiet!"

"Josh Pinto, where are you taking us?" Ruth Rose demanded. "I'm all scratches! Why didn't you tell us

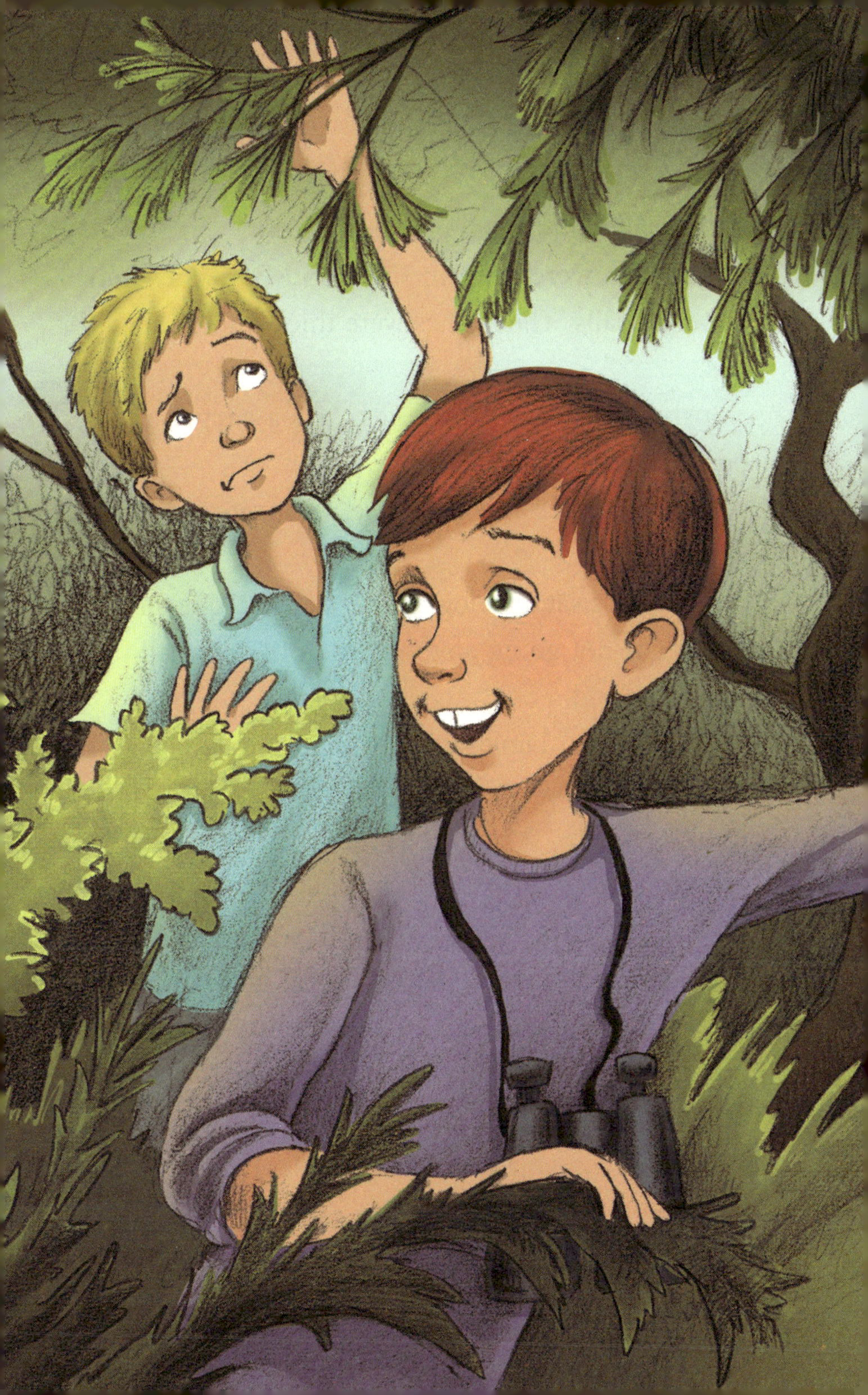

we'd be walking through pricker bushes?"

The kids were deep in the woods, not far from the horse trails. The bushes were thick under the tall trees.

Josh grinned at his friends. "It's a surprise," he said. "Trust me, you'll love it."

"Well, I don't love all these mosquitoes," Dink muttered.

Ruth Rose sat on a log and scratched a bite on her ankle. "I'm not going any farther until you spill the beans," she said.

"Me neither," Dink said. He plopped down next to Ruth Rose. "Out with it, Josh. Why'd you drag us into this jungle?"

"And what's with the binoculars?" Ruth Rose asked.

"Okay, I'll tell you." Josh squeezed between them on the log and pulled a piece of paper from his pocket. He spread it out across his knees.

It was a drawing of a bird. It had dark feathers, a curved beak, and black markings under the eyes.

"What is it?" asked Dink. "An eagle?"

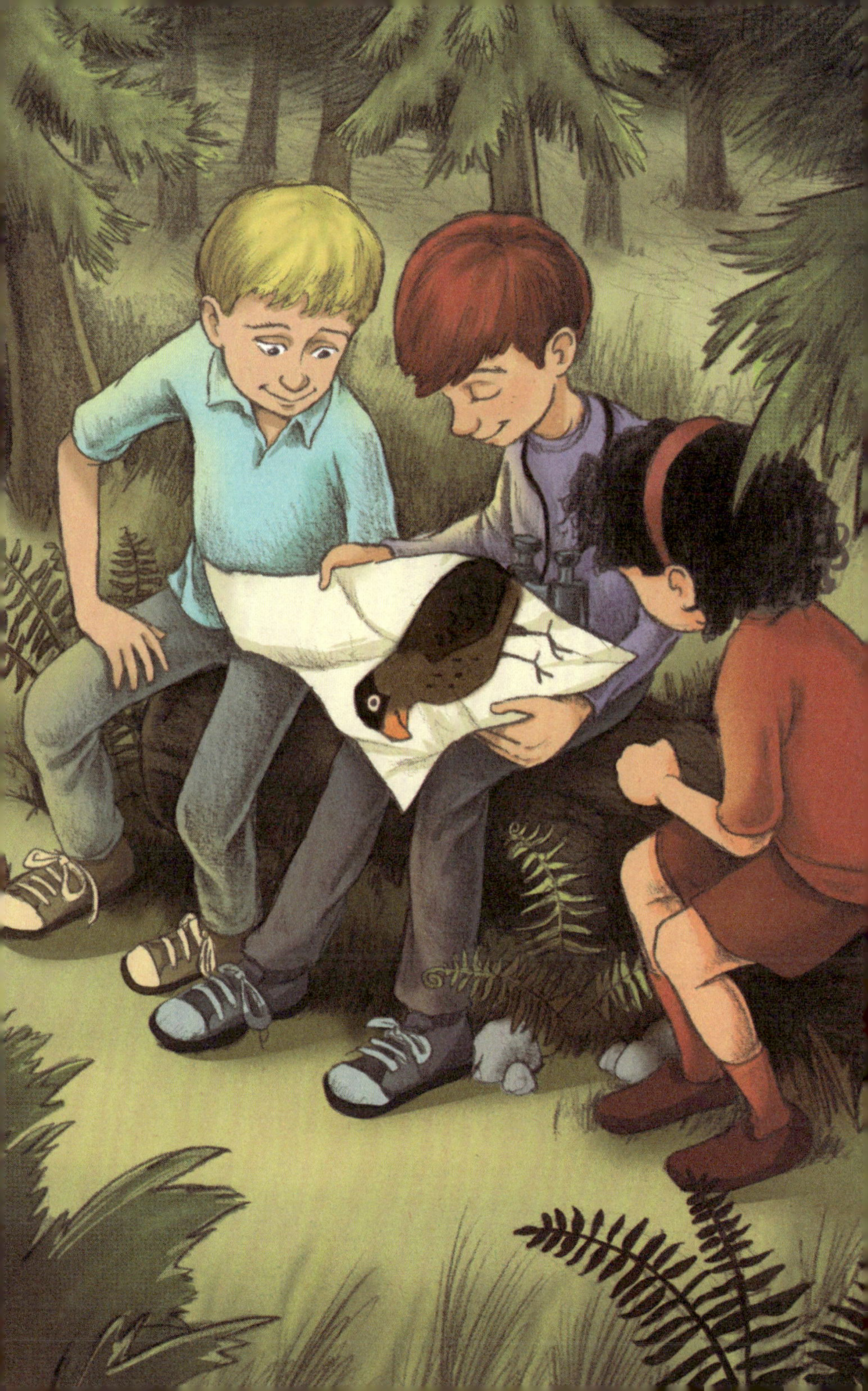

Josh shook his head. "No, it's a peregrine falcon. They were almost extinct—but now there's a family in Green Lawn!"

Dink was impressed. "Did you draw this?"

Josh nodded. "Yup. I found a nest with three babies. I've been watching them for a couple of weeks now."

"And you're just telling us today?" Ruth Rose said. "Thanks for sharing, Josh."

Josh folded the drawing and stuck it in his pocket. "Falcons don't like to be disturbed," he said. "I was waiting to tell you when the babies were older."

Dink looked over their heads at the trees. "So where's the nest?" he asked.

Josh stood up. "We're almost there," he said.

The kids picked their way through the undergrowth. Between the branches, Dink could see glimpses of the Indian River.

A minute later, Josh stopped. "It's right over there," he whispered. "The tall tree in the clearing."

"All I see are leaves," Ruth Rose said.

Josh pointed about halfway up the tree. "See that

brown stuff right over the dead branch?"

"I see it!" Ruth Rose cried.

"Me too," Dink said. "How did you climb up there?"

"I didn't," said Josh. "If you disturb the nest, the parents might abandon the babies."

Josh pointed to a white birch tree at the edge of the clearing. "I climb that tree and look over with my binoculars."

"Can we climb up and take a look?" Ruth Rose asked.

"Sure," Josh said. "Only we have to be quiet. I don't want to scare them."

The birch tree was perfect for climbing. The smooth limbs made a natural ladder. Dink and Ruth Rose followed Josh up to a thick branch.

Josh trained his binoculars on the other tree. He adjusted the focus by turning a little wheel between the two eyepieces.

"That's weird," he muttered.

"What's weird?" Ruth Rose asked.

"Let me see." Dink took the glasses and squinted through the lenses. From his perch, Dink could see directly into the nest. It was woven of twigs, pine needles, and bits of dead leaves.

But there weren't any falcons. All Dink could see was a few feathers.

He looked at Josh with raised eyebrows.

"Where are they?" he asked.

"What's going on?" Ruth Rose asked.

Josh looked at her. "The baby falcons are gone."

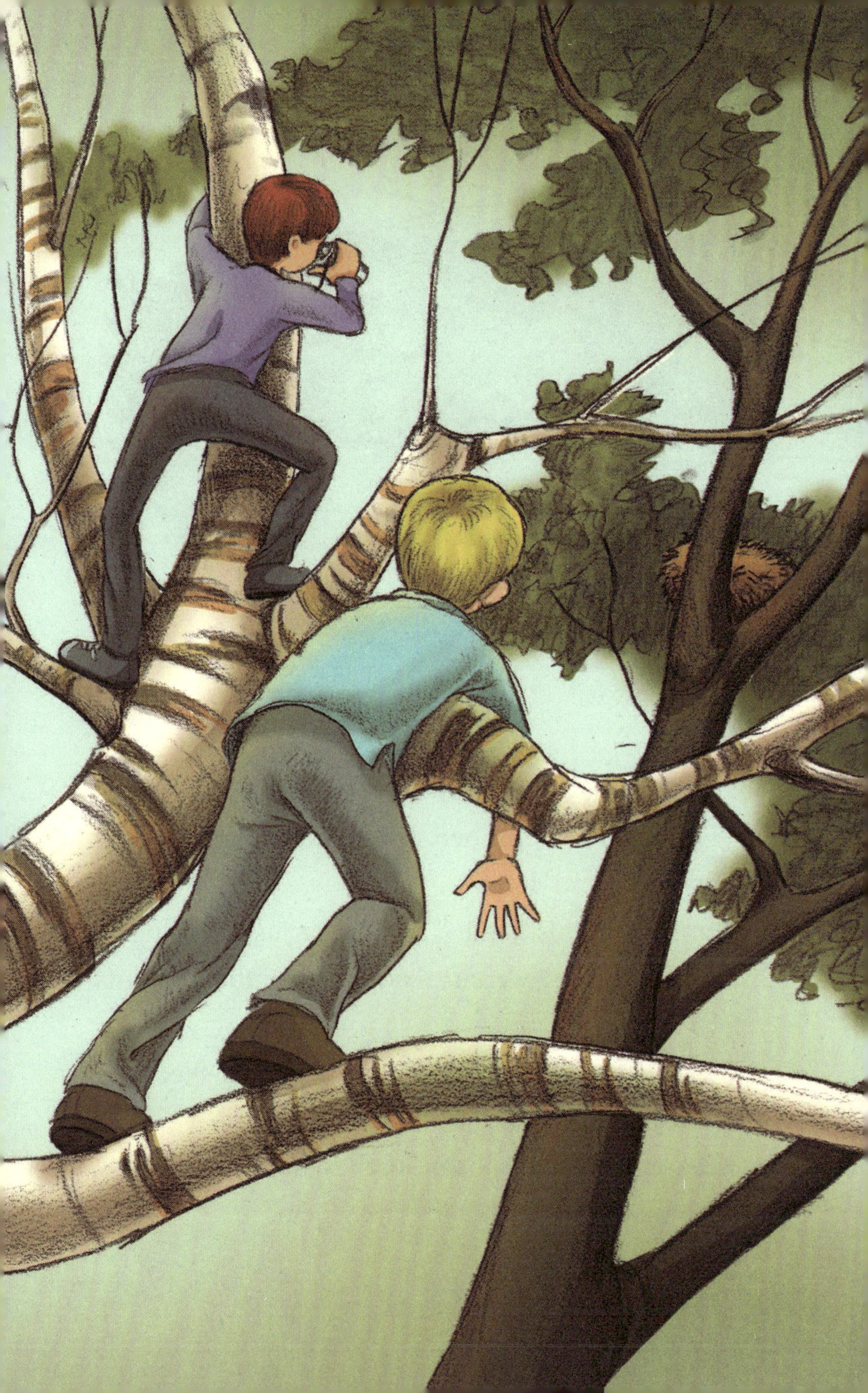

Chapter 2

"Maybe they flew away," Ruth Rose suggested.

The kids had climbed down and were standing under the falcons' tree.

Josh shook his head. "They were just learning to fly," he said. "They weren't ready to leave their parents yet."

"Could they have fallen out?" Dink asked. He glanced at the ground.

"I doubt it," said Josh. "If they had, the parents would still be here, watching over them."

He frowned. "I think something took those birds," he said.

"What do you mean?" Ruth Rose asked. "What kind of something?"

"Animals," Josh explained. "Owls and snakes like to eat baby birds."

"But wouldn't the parents protect the little falcons?" Dink asked.

"Yeah," Josh said. "Unless something happened to them, too."

"Maybe something scared the parents away," Ruth Rose said.

Josh shook his head. "The parents wouldn't leave their babies."

"Then what could have happened to them?" Dink asked. "Five falcons can't just disappear!"

"I don't know," Josh said. He looked worried. "Come on, let's get out of here. I want to report this."

"Report it to who?" Ruth Rose asked. She and Dink followed Josh back toward the path.

"I'm not sure. But we can ask Mrs. Wong," said Josh. "She knows a lot about animals."

A to Z 神秘案件

Twenty minutes later, the kids walked into Furry Feet, Mrs. Wong's pet shop. She was cleaning a large goldfish tank.

"Hi, kids," Mrs. Wong said. "What's up? I was just about to close for the day."

Josh explained about the missing falcons. "They were there yesterday," he said, "but today they're gone!"

Mrs. Wong wiped her hands on her jeans. "That does seem odd," she said.

"Peregrines are an endangered species," Josh said. "Should I report this to someone?"

"That's a good idea, Josh," said Mrs. Wong. She went over to her desk and pulled open a drawer.

"Here you go," she said, handing Josh a card. "That's the number for the Department of Environmental Protection—the DEP, for short. They have an office over at the fire station."

"Thanks, Mrs. Wong," Josh said. "May I use your phone?"

Josh dialed the number while Mrs. Wong went back to cleaning the goldfish tank.

游隼的羽毛

Dink and Ruth Rose listened as Josh explained about the nest and the missing falcons. He thanked whomever he was speaking with and hung up.

"Someone is gonna go out there and take a look," he told Dink and Ruth Rose. "But the guy I talked to said an owl probably got the babies."

Ruth Rose shuddered. "Those poor falcons!"

The kids thanked Mrs. Wong and left the store.

Outside, it was starting to get dark. Ruth Rose, Josh, and Dink crossed Main Street and cut through Center Park. A family of ducks was swimming in the pond. When the parents noticed the humans, they quacked loudly to their babies. The ducklings quickly swam over to their mother and father.

Josh stopped walking. "I don't think an owl could have taken those baby falcons."

"You don't?" Dink asked.

Josh shook his head. "Mother and father falcons are fierce! They wouldn't let an owl within ten feet of their nest."

"Could a snake climb that high?" Ruth Rose asked.

A to Z 神秘案件

Josh smirked. "Yeah, a human snake!"

"What do you mean?" Dink asked. "You think a person stole the falcons?" Josh nodded.

游隼的羽毛

"But who would do something like that?" Ruth Rose asked.

"I don't know," Josh said. "But we're going to find out!"

Chapter 3

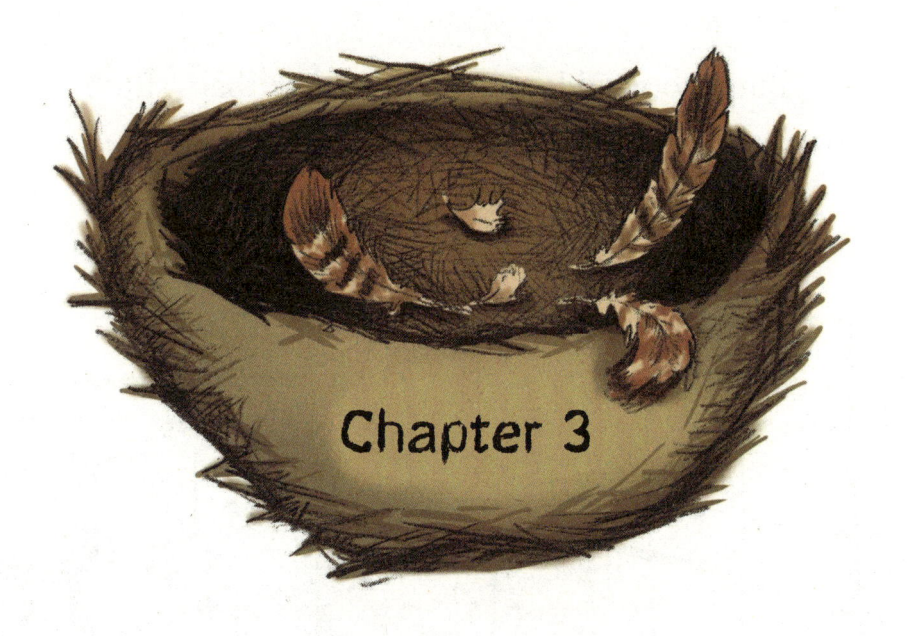

The next morning, Dink rang Ruth Rose's doorbell. She came to the door wearing a green jogging suit. Even her sneakers and headband were green.

"You look like a bush," Dink said.

Ruth Rose grinned and yelled into the house, "MOM, I'M LEAVING!"

She and Dink headed up Woody Street to pick up Josh. They were going back to the falcons' nest to look for clues.

Josh lived at the end of Farm Lane, in a big yellow house. Behind the house stood a white barn. Josh was shooting baskets at a hoop nailed to the barn door.

He was dressed in a camouflage shirt and pants.

"Geez," Dink said, "why didn't you guys tell me you were going disguised as trees!"

The three kids hurried down River Road, then took a bike path into the woods. Just before they reached the clearing, Josh stopped. A man wearing jeans and a flannel shirt was standing under the falcons' tree, looking up into the branches.

The kids looked at each other, then stepped into the clearing.

The man turned around. He had wavy black hair, a tanned face, and blue eyes.

"Hi there," the man said. "What are you kids up to?"

"We were just hiking," Josh said cautiously.

The man smiled. "Wait a minute. Your voice is awfully familiar. Are you the guy who called my office yesterday about the missing falcons?"

Josh grinned. "Yeah, that was me," he said. Josh introduced himself. "And these are my friends, Dink and Ruth Rose."

A to Z 神秘案件

"Very nice to meet you," the man said. "My name's Curt. Look, guys, I know you want to help, but the best thing you can do is to stay away from here. The adult falcons won't come back if they see or smell you kids."

"But we came back to look for clues," Josh said. "I thought a person might have taken the falcons."

Curt looked surprised. "A person? Well, it's

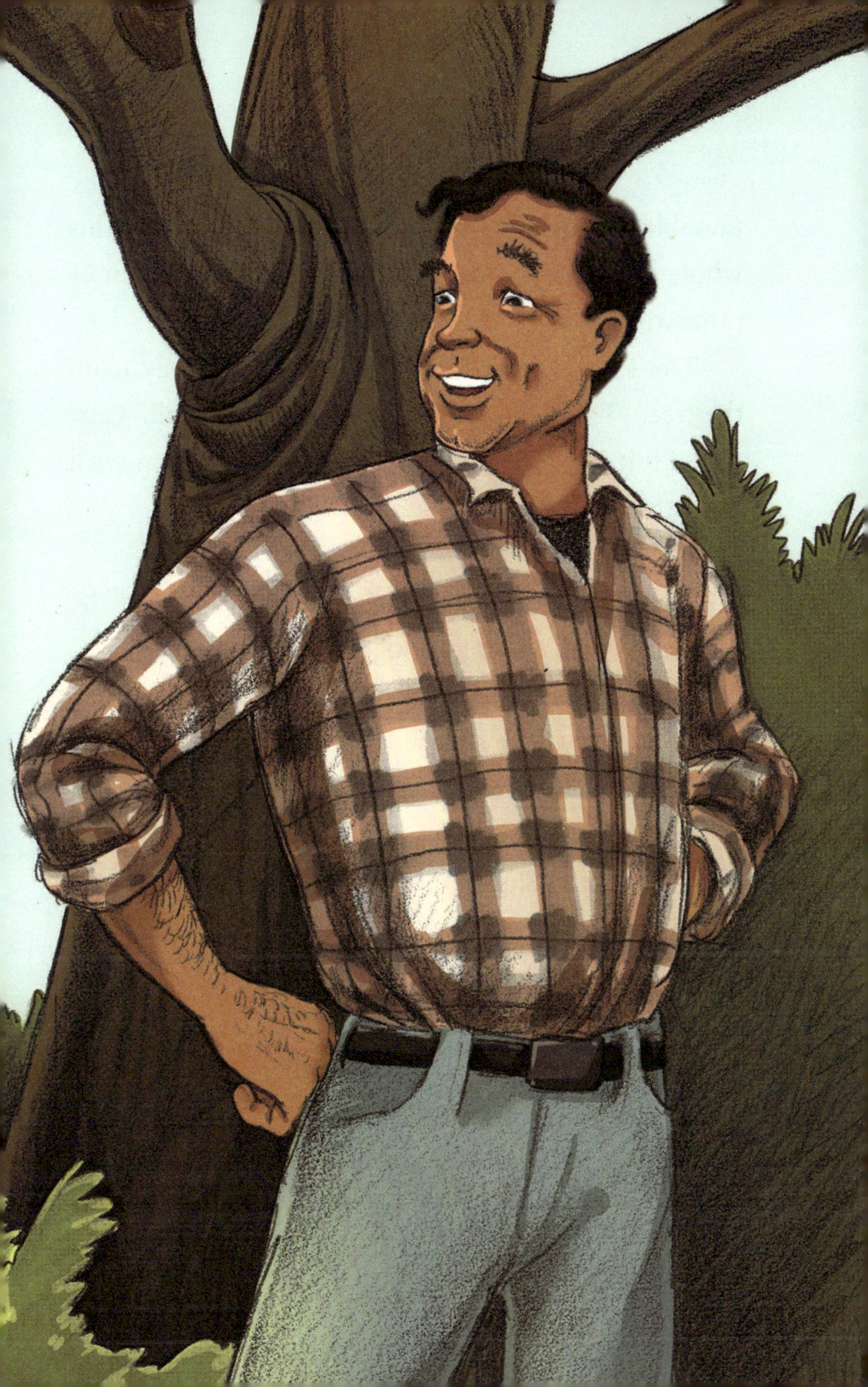

possible, I suppose. But I doubt it. I've been over this whole area, and I didn't find a single clue, human or otherwise."

The kids followed Curt as he walked away from the tree. "The DEP appreciates your phone call," Curt said, "but leave the rest to us. I have a feeling we'll wrap this up soon."

At the trail, Curt turned right. "Thanks again!" he said. He waved and began jogging down the path.

The kids headed down the trail in the other direction. Suddenly, Josh stopped. "Listen!" he said.

"What?" Ruth Rose said.

"I heard something." Josh knelt next to a patch of tangled weeds. Slowly, he parted the stalks with his fingers.

A brown bird was hunched in the weeds. It had a sharp beak and shiny black eyes.

"It's a young peregrine falcon!" Josh said. "He must be from the nest!"

The bird was trembling. It opened its beak and made cack-cack-cack noises at Josh. Its shiny eyes never left Josh's face.

"The poor thing looks scared," Ruth Rose said.

Josh took off his T-shirt and carefully draped it over the bird. "He won't be so scared if he can't see us," Josh explained. He held the bundle against this chest.

"What should we do with it?" Dink asked.

"We can't leave him here," Josh said. "Something will eat him."

"Let's take him to Mrs. Wong!" Ruth Rose said.

The kids hurried down the path. Josh smoothed the bird's feathers and spoke to it in a soothing voice.

"Hey, what's this?" Josh said. He gently stretched out one of the falcon's legs.

Wrapped around the leg was a narrow metal band.

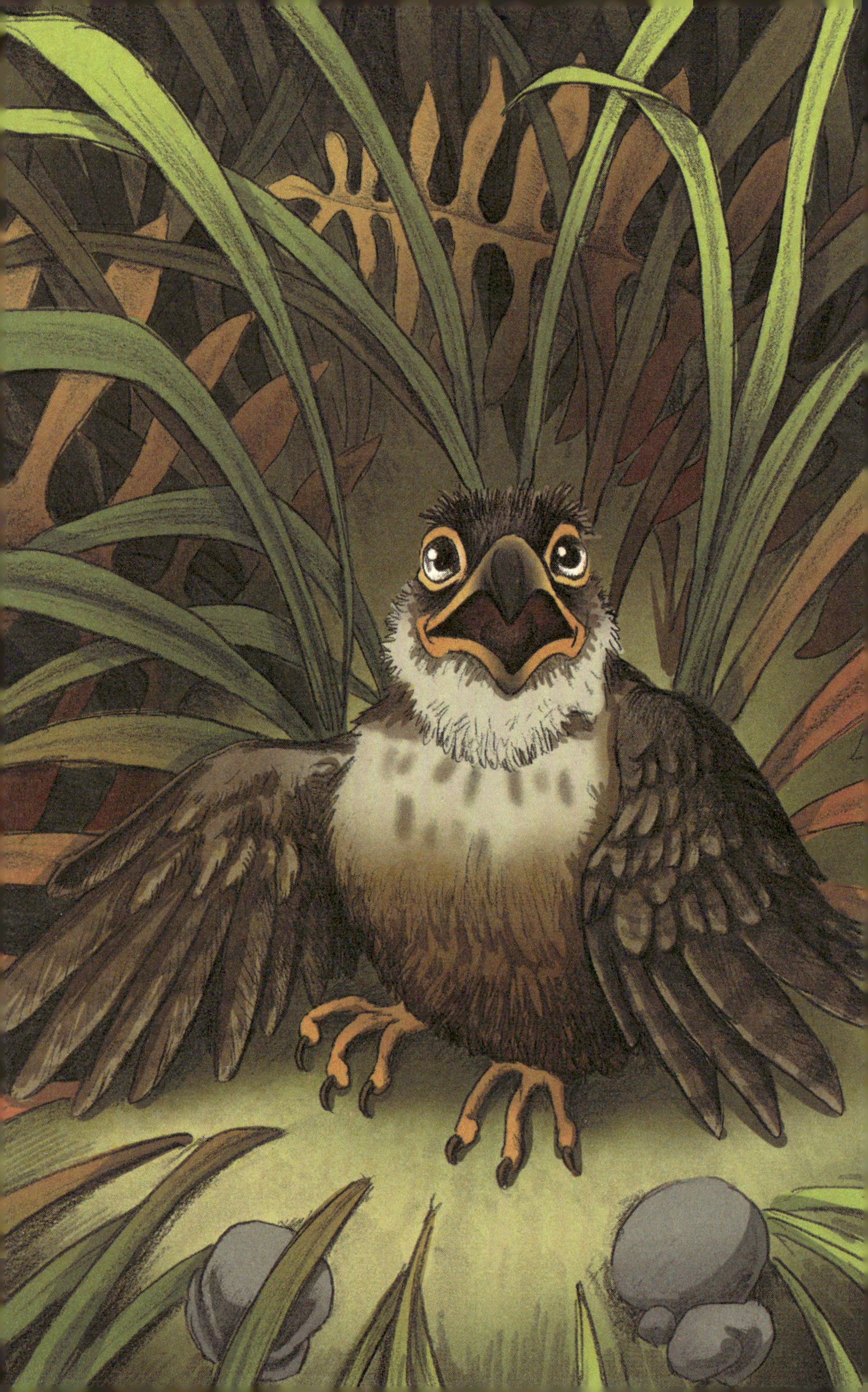

Chapter 4

Mrs. Wong examined the band. "There's writing on it," she told the kids. "But it's too small for me to read."

"What is it?" Josh asked.

"It's a name tag," said Mrs. Wong. "Just like you'd hang on a dog's collar. Someone thinks he owns this bird."

Josh was holding the falcon, still partly wrapped in his T-shirt. It sat quietly, watching the humans.

"I wonder if he's hungry," Ruth Rose said. "What

do falcons eat?"

"Peregrines mostly eat other birds," Josh said. "But they'll eat fish and other stuff, too."

"Let's find out!" said Mrs. Wong. She opened a small refrigerator and pulled out some raw hamburger. She pinched off a chunk and held it under the falcon's beak.

"Come on, take it," Josh murmured.

Suddenly, the falcon's head shot forward. In one quick gulp, the meat was gone.

"Boy, I guess he was hungry!" Ruth Rose said. "We should name him Flash!"

Flash began making a loud, piercing call. He shrieked over and over until Mrs. Wong fed him another piece of hamburger meat. After the second helping, he stopped fussing and closed his eyes.

"What should we do with him?" Josh asked Mrs. Wong.

She reached for the phone. "For starters, we should ask Doc Henry to look him over."

The kids listened as Mrs. Wong told the veterinarian about Flash. She hung up the phone and said,

"He'll take a look if you kids bring the bird to his office. He's right over on East Green Street."

Josh bundled Flash into his shirt again, and the kids hurried to Doc Henry's office.

While Josh washed his hands, Doc Henry examined Flash. "And you found this guy where?" Doc Henry asked.

"Out in the woods," Josh said, pulling his shirt back on. He explained how they'd gone to see the young falcons, only to find the nest empty.

"Well, this is a young peregrine, all right," the vet said. "Pretty rare around here."

Doc found the band on Flash's leg and cut it off. Then he gently spread the falcon's wings and probed for broken bones.

"He seems healthy enough," Doc said. "Probably just starting to fly. But lookee here. Someone's trimmed his wing feathers!"

The kids crowded around.

"See?" the vet continued. "Peregrines normally have long, pointy wings. These have been rounded off with scissors."

Just then, a tall woman with black hair came up to the table. "What's everyone looking at?" she asked.

"Oh, hi, Grace," Doc said. "Kids, this is my new assistant, Grace Lockwood. Grace, these kids brought in a young peregrine."

The woman gave the kids a long look. Her eyes were piercing. They reminded Dink of an eagle's eyes.

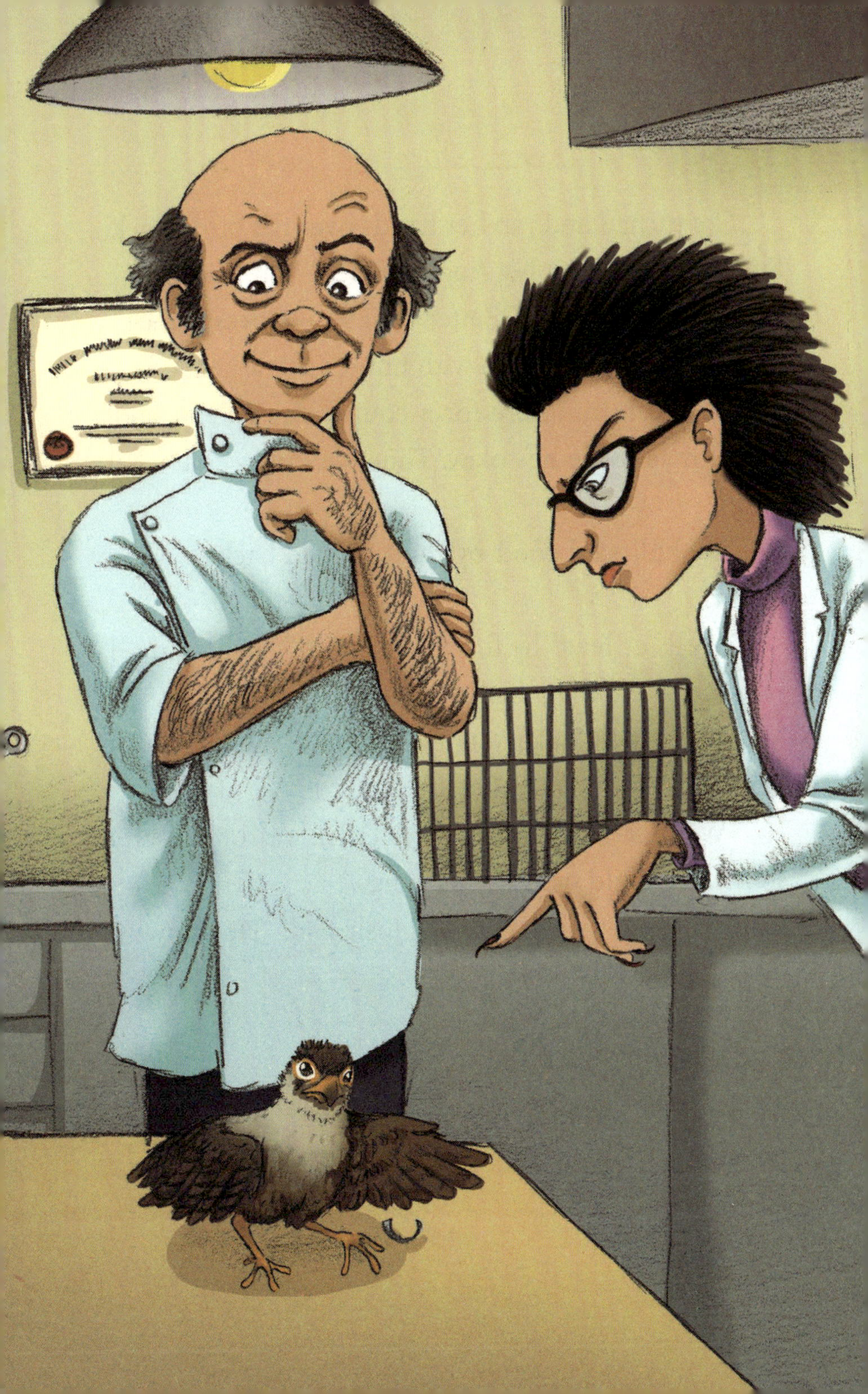

She turned and ran her hands over the bird's back. Suddenly, Flash bit her finger. "Ouch!" she said.

The vet chuckled. "Better wear your gloves, Grace."

"What should we do with him?" Josh asked.

"I'll keep him here for a couple days," Doc said. "We'll make sure he's okay. Then we can decide what to do."

The kids said good-bye and headed back to Main Street.

"Well, at least he'll be safe there," Josh said. "I wonder where the other two are."

"Wherever Flash was before he escaped!" Ruth Rose said.

"What I want to know," Dink said, "is why someone would trim Flash's wings."

"Why don't we ask Curt?" Josh said. "He knows a lot about falcons."

Chapter 5

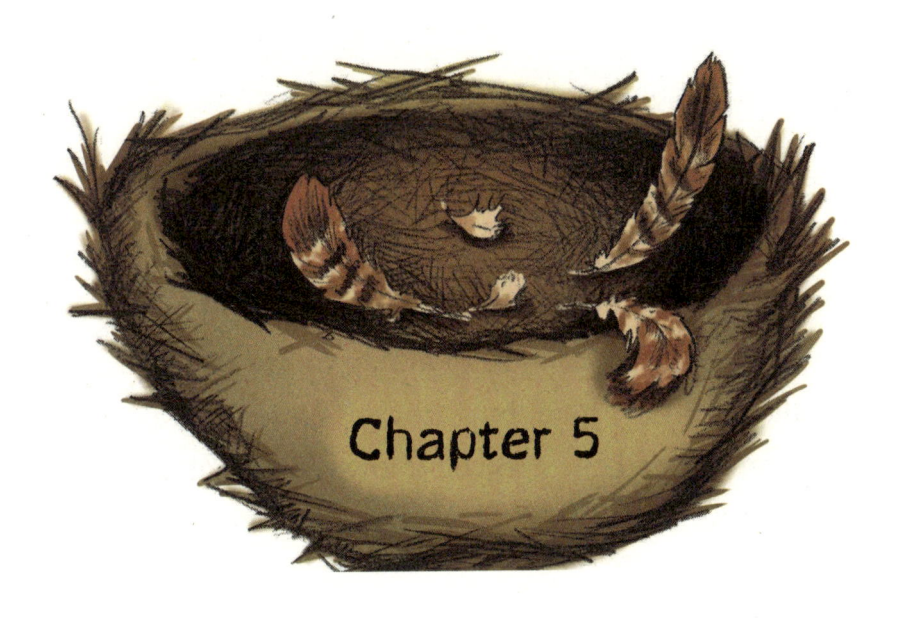

A small sign on the side of the fire station said DEP—DOWNSTAIRS. A green arrow pointed the way. At the bottom of the stairs, the kids came to a door that said DEPARTMENT OF ENVIRONMENTAL PROTECTION.

No one was in the office. There were a few desks and a bunch of file cabinets against one wall. A stuffed owl in a glass case stood on a counter.

Just then, the door opened and a woman dressed in a T-shirt and tan shorts walked in. "Can I help you?" she asked the kids.

"We're looking for Curt," Josh said.

"Mr. Striker usually goes home to eat lunch," she said. "Do you want to come back later?"

"It's kind of important," Josh said. "Does he live in Green Lawn? We could walk over."

The woman pointed to a map of the town on the wall. "He's new here, but I think he's renting a cabin out on Bridge Lane. Do you know where that is?"

"Sure," Dink said. "He must live near the river, right?"

The woman nodded. "That's right. Just look for his brown pickup truck."

The kids left the fire station and hiked over to Bridge Lane. There were only a few houses in this part of town. Most of them were surrounded by trees and thick shrubbery.

"That must be it," Josh said. They were standing in front of a wooden fence near a group of pine trees. A gravel driveway cut through the trees, leading to a small cabin.

"Look, there's a brown truck," Dink said.

When the kids walked through the gate, they saw

游隼的羽毛

Curt Striker sitting on the cabin's small porch. He was eating a sandwich.

Curt jumped down off the porch and headed toward them. "Hi, kids," he said. "What brings you way out here?"

119

Josh told him about how they'd found one of the baby falcons in the woods.

"Not only that," Ruth Rose said, "someone put a tag on his leg and clipped his wings!"

"Really?" Curt said. He looked thoughtful. "Sounds

like I owe you an apology, Josh. A person did take that falcon."

Josh grinned shyly.

"Why would someone clip his wings?" Dink asked.

"Well," Curt said, "the most likely reason is that someone was training him to do something."

"Like what?" asked Ruth Rose.

Curt shrugged. "Could have been a lot of different things."

While they talked, Curt walked them back toward Bridge Lane. "Where is this falcon now?" he asked.

"We took him to the vet," Josh said. "Doc Henry said he'd take care of him."

Curt nodded. "Thanks for letting me know. I'll be sure to check in with Doc Henry."

The kids said good-bye and headed back toward Main Street.

"I hope he catches whoever took those falcons," Ruth Rose said. "Cutting a bird's feathers off is just plain mean!"

Josh nodded. "Yeah, but at least it doesn't hurt. I think it's like cutting your toenails."

They walked past Ellie's Diner. Grace Lockwood was sitting at the window, reading and eating lunch. When she noticed the kids watching her, she stared

游隼的羽毛

back at them through the glass.

Her face was blank, but her eyes made the kids hurry away.

"She looks upset about something," Ruth Rose said.

"Maybe she just doesn't like kids gawking at her while she eats," Dink said.

"Did you guys see what she was reading?" Josh asked.

"Some magazine," Dink said.

"Not just some magazine," Josh said, looking at Dink and Ruth Rose. "I recognized the cover. It was *FALCONRY TODAY.*"

Chapter 6

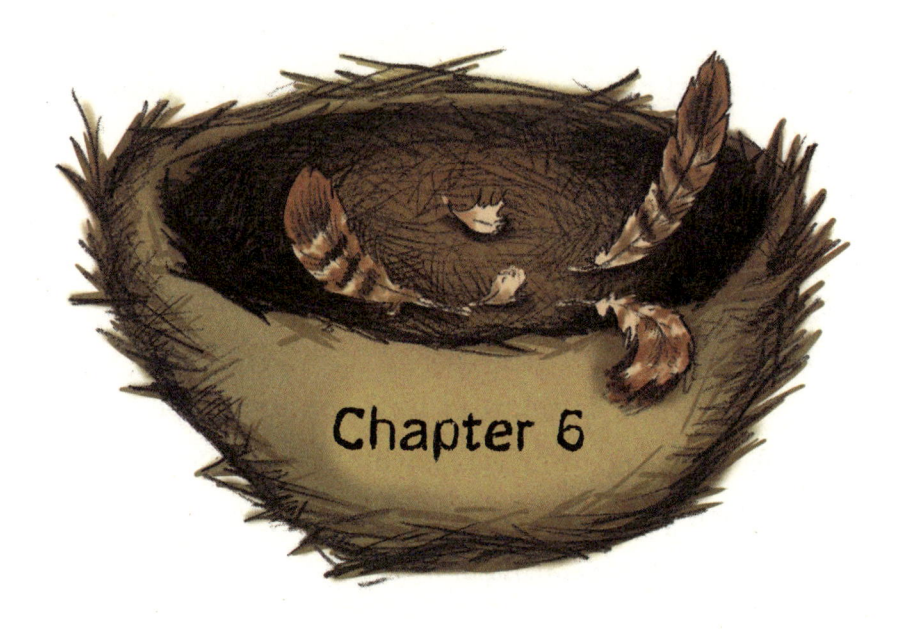

"I think Josh is sick," Ruth Rose whispered to Dink.

"I am not sick," Josh said. He took another bite of his tuna sandwich.

The kids were eating lunch at Dink's picnic table.

"Then why are you so quiet?" Ruth Rose asked. "You haven't insulted me all day!"

Josh chewed his sandwich. "I'll insult you later," he said. "Right now I'm thinking about those missing falcons." He looked at his friends. "I think Grace Lockwood took them."

125

A to Z 神秘案件

"Grace Lockwood!" Dink said. "Why do you think it was her?"

"You saw that magazine she was reading," Josh said. "It was all about falcons."

Ruth Rose nodded. "She was acting a little strange at Doc Henry's."

"Yeah, and remember how she looked at us at Ellie's," Josh said. "She was staring right at me."

"Staring at you?" Dink said. "Josh, she stared at us because we were staring at her!"

Josh snitched one of Ruth Rose's carrot sticks. "Let's go back to the vet's and talk to her," he said. "Maybe she'll say something that'll be a clue!"

Dink got up to go. "Okay, but I think you're wrong, Josh. Just because Grace Lockwood reads magazines about falcons doesn't mean she goes around robbing nests."

At the vet's, the kids peered through the window at Grace Lockwood.

"Look!" Josh whispered. "She's wearing long leather gloves! Falconer swear gloves like that!"

126

"So do firefighters," Dink said.

They went inside. Grace Lockwood was holding a crow down on a table. The bird had plastic wrapped around its leg and neck.

She looked up. "Yes?" she asked.

"Um, we came to see how Flash is doing," Ruth Rose said. "What happened to the crow?"

Grace shook her head. "Plastic six-pack holders!"

The kids watched as Grace carefully snipped the plastic with scissors.

The crow bit her gloves several times. Dink shuddered. That beak looked sharp!

When the crow was untangled, Grace moved toward the rear of the building. "Will one of you get the door for me?"

Dink opened the door and held it. Grace carried the crow through a small courtyard that was filled with cages and pens.

She threw the black bird into the air. "And stay away from plastic!" she yelled. The crow disappeared into the trees.

Dink looked around the yard. It was as big as a

basketball court and surrounded by a tall wooden fence with a gate.

Dink saw a sleeping skunk in one cage. Other cages held raccoons and rabbits. He saw a few snakes and a lot of birds. He even saw a baby fox!

"I always thought vets just took care of cats and dogs," Josh said.

"Some do," Grace said. "I happen to like wildlife."

Josh looked at Dink and Ruth Rose and wiggled his eyebrows.

"Where's Flash?" Josh asked, looking around at several other cages.

"I put him over here," she said, walking toward a corner of the courtyard. "Doc likes to separate the newcomers from the other animals."

Grace stopped in front of a cage covered by a small rug. "He may be sleeping," she said.

She removed the rug. The bottom of the cage was covered with straw. Inside was a section of hollow log.

"That's where he goes to hide from us," Grace said. She tapped lightly on the side of the cage.

"That's strange," she said, opening the cage door.

游隼的羽毛

She jiggled the log, then peered inside.

"What's the matter?" Ruth Rose asked.

"He's gone," Grace said.

Chapter 7

"What!" Josh looked into the cage. "How could Flash be gone?"

"I don't know," Grace said. "I'd better tell Doc."

She hurried toward the office.

"Something's fishy here," Ruth Rose said. "How could Flash just disappear?"

"Someone stole him again!" Josh said.

Doc Henry and Grace ran across the courtyard. The vet was peeling off a pair of surgical gloves.

"He was in his cage before lunch," Grace said.

Doc Henry bent over and looked into the cage. "Darndest thing," he muttered. "Was the gate locked?"

Grace nodded. "I think so, but I'll check." She ran to a corner of the courtyard. "The lock's been busted!"

Doc and the kids hurried over. The thick wooden gate was closed, but the lock had been shattered. Bits of wood and metal were on the ground.

Doc Henry picked up the pieces of the lock. "Somebody sure wanted to get in here," he said. "That lock was the best on the market!"

Dink examined the door closely. "I wonder if there are any fingerprints on the wood," he said.

"Could be," the vet said.

"Should we call Officer Fallon?" Dink asked.

"That's an excellent suggestion," Doc Henry said. He walked back toward his office.

"I'd better get that lock fixed," Grace said. She hurried away without saying good-bye.

The kids left. They walked past Crystal Pond back toward Main Street.

"I'll bet Grace busted that lock to make it look like

someone broke in," Josh said.

Dink shook his head. "Grace helps animals, Josh."

"Do birds have memories?" Ruth Rose asked suddenly.

"Why?" Dink asked.

"Well, remember when we first brought Flash to Doc Henry's office? Flash bit Grace on the hand."

"Yeah, so?"

Ruth Rose stopped walking and looked at Dink and Josh. "Well, if Grace climbed the tree and took those falcons, maybe Flash remembers her. Maybe that's why he bit her!"

"You guys are jumping to conclusions," Dink said. He pushed the cross button at Main Street.

"I think we need more information about peregrine falcons," he added.

"Dink's right," Ruth Rose told Josh. "If we know more about them, maybe we'll be able to figure out why someone's taking them."

"Why don't we go to the library?" Dink suggested, crossing Main Street.

"Okay," Josh said, "but Grace Lockwood is still at

游隼的羽毛

the top of my list!"

"Who else is on your list?" Ruth Rose asked.

Josh jogged across the street. "Nobody!"

Chapter 8

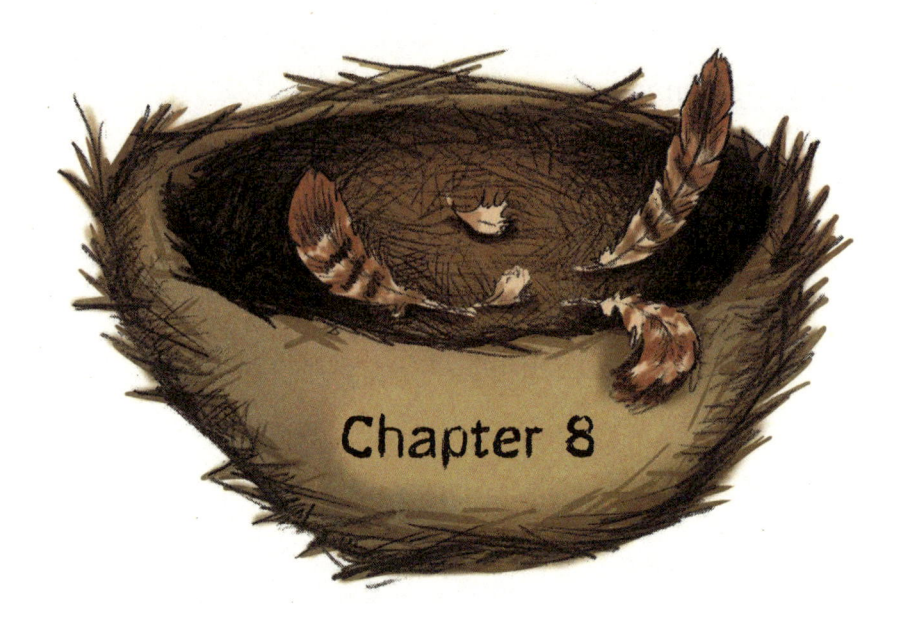

When the kids entered the library, Mrs. Mackleroy was gluing a cover onto a book.

"Hi, kids," she said. "Someone loves this book so much they wore the binding right off!"

She finished the job, then laid a heavy book on top of the glued one to keep it flat. "There," she said, wiping glue from her fingers. "So how can I help you today?"

"We're looking for information about falcons," Josh told her.

Mrs. Mackleroy pointed to the computer table. "Do you know how to do a computer search?" she asked.

"Sure, we do it in school all the time," Ruth Rose said. "Come on, guys!"

Dink sat at the computer. Josh and Ruth Rose looked over his shoulder. Dink typed in F-A-L-C-O-N-S, then hit the "enter" key.

A few seconds later, a long list of book titles appeared on the screen.

"Geez, there must be fifty books about falcons," Josh said.

"Try PEREGRINE," Ruth Rose said. Dink typed in the new word, and the list shortened. The library had four books about peregrine falcons.

Dink printed the shorter list, and they took it to Mrs. Mackleroy.

"These are in the children's room," she said, making check marks next to two of the titles.

The kids found one of the two books. The title was *Peregrine Falcons:Royal Raptors*. They huddled together on a bench and quickly turned pages.

The book talked about how peregrine falcons had nearly been wiped out because of pesticides.

They flipped more pages until they came to "Amazing Falcon Facts."

"Peregrine falcons are easy to train," Josh read aloud.

"And look, it says they mate for life," Ruth Rose added.

"Look at fact number seven," Dink said, running his finger down the page. "Peregrine falcons are

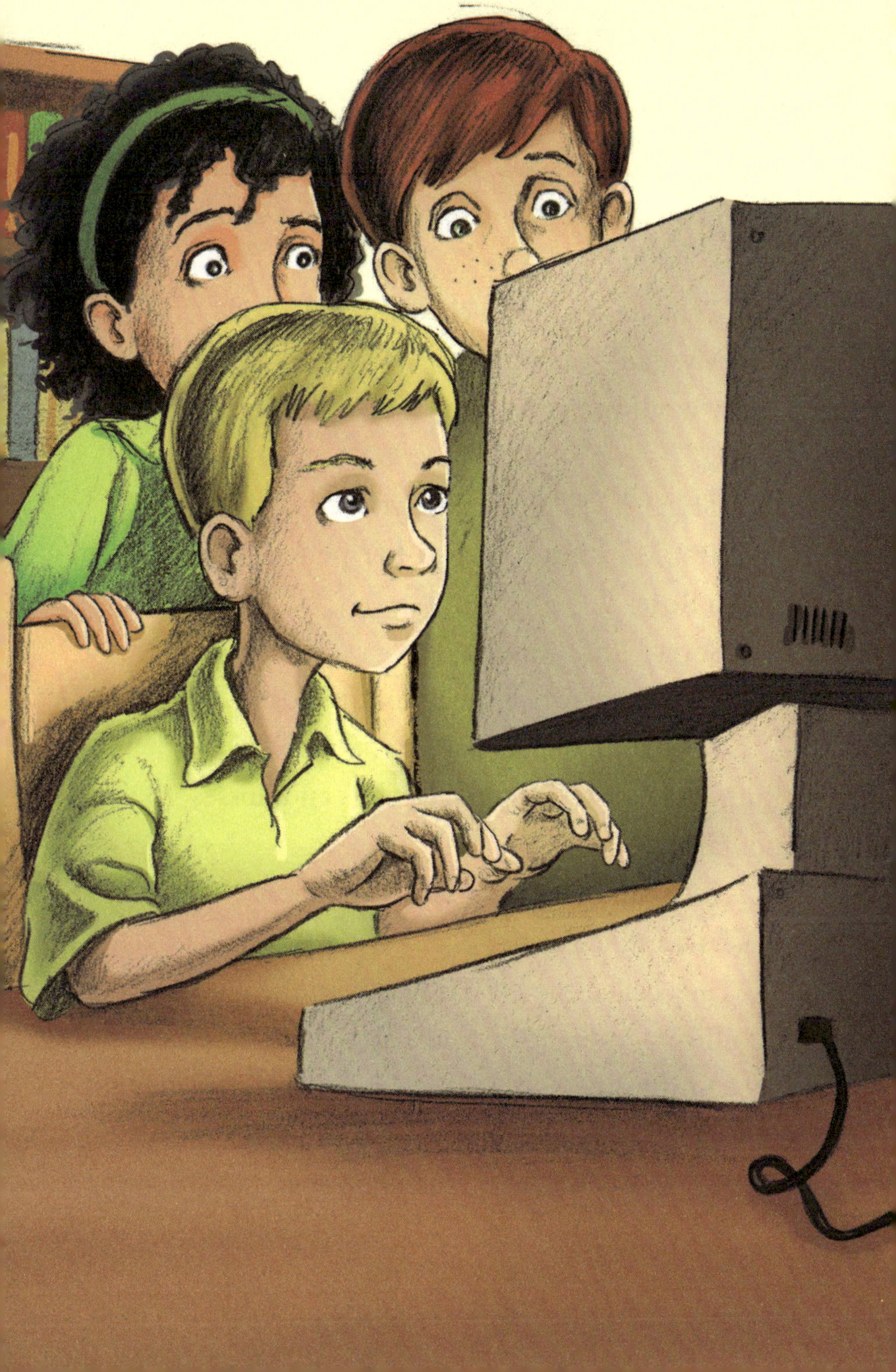

among nature's fastest hunters. When chasing birds, peregrines have been known to top 200miles per hour!"

"That's faster than a cheetah!" Josh said.

"My dad's car only goes a hundred," Dink said. "Boy, wouldn't it be neat to see peregrine falcons racing."

"THAT'S IT!" Ruth Rose yelled.

Mrs. Mackleroy tapped her pencil on her desk. "Ruth Rose…"

"Sorry," Ruth Rose said.

The kids returned the book and hurried outside.

"I bet someone is stealing falcons to race them!" Ruth Rose said. "People race dogs and horses, so why not falcons?"

"Let's tell Curt," Josh said. "He doesn't even know Flash was stolen again."

They called the DEP office from the phone booth in Ellie's Diner. Josh told Curt that someone had broken into the vet's and stolen Flash. Then he told him about what they had learned in the library.

A few seconds later, Josh hung up. "He's coming

right over."

"He is?" Dink said.

"Yeah," Josh said. "And while we're waiting, I could use a pistachio cone!"

Ruth Rose ordered her usual:strawberry. Dink got his favorite, butter crunch. The kids sat in a booth and worked on their cones.

"You know, I've been thinking," Ruth Rose said between licks. "Who besides us knew that Flash was at the vet's?"

Dink and Josh looked at her. "Well, Mrs. Wong knew," Dink said.

"For sure, she didn't break in and steal Flash!" Josh said.

"And Doc Henry knew, but I don't think it's him, either," Dink said.

Ruth Rose glanced at her friends. "Who else?"

"Grace Lockwood!" Josh said.

"Don't forget about Curt," Dink said. "We told him that Flash was at Doc Henry's."

Josh shook his head. "It's Curt's job to protect wildlife."

Just then, Curt Striker walked into the diner. He ordered a cup of coffee, then slid into the booth. "So you kids have been doing some detective work, eh?" he said.

"Someone stole Flash right out of the vet's place!" Ruth Rose told Curt.

"I know," Curt said. "Josh told me on the phone. But who's Flash?"

She grinned. "The falcon! We named him that because he eats so fast."

"So what's this about racing falcons?" Curt said, looking at Josh.

"Well, we read that peregrine falcons can fly 200 miles an hour!" Josh said. "So we thought someone might be training them to race."

Curt sipped his coffee. "Racing falcons, eh? That's an interesting idea."

"Could someone make money racing falcons," Dink asked Curt, "like in a horse race?"

Curt nodded slowly. "Yes, I guess they could."

He finished his coffee. "Tell you what, let me run your idea by a few of my contacts. Meanwhile, let's just keep this between us, okay?"

"Do you really think you can find out who took the falcons?" Ruth Rose said.

Curt slid out of his seat. "You can count on it," he said.

Chapter 9

The kids stepped outside Ellie's and saw Officer Fallon standing on the corner.

"Hi, kids," he said. "What're you doing on such a nice day?"

"Hi, Officer Fallon," Dink said. "Did Doc Henry call you about the break-in?"

Officer Fallon pushed the "walk" button on a traffic light pole. He was carrying a small black case. "I was just heading over there with my fingerprint kit," he said. "The doc told me about these disappearing falcons. But how are you kids involved?"

Josh filled him in on how he'd been watching the falcons' nest.

"When we went to look yesterday, the falcons were gone," Ruth Rose said.

"And we think we know who did it!" Josh said.

Interrupting each other, Josh and Ruth Rose explained how they thought Grace Lockwood was stealing falcons and training them to race.

"Well, I don't think it's her," Dink said.

Officer Fallon nodded slowly. "I tell you what," he said. "When we get there, let's just watch and listen." He smiled. "Maybe we'll all learn something."

Officer Fallon and the kids walked into Doc Henry's outer office. Through the window, they could see him and Grace putting a cast on a dog's leg.

"It would be neat to be a vet," Josh said. "You get to play with animals all day."

"It's not play, Josh, it's hard work," Officer Fallon said. "Some vets get called out in the middle of the night! Besides, I thought you wanted to be a bird artist."

Josh grinned. "Couldn't I do both?"

Doc Henry came out, wiping white plaster dust from his fingers. "Thanks for coming over," he said to Officer Fallon. "Come on, I'll show you what's left of my lock."

The kids watched Grace lift the dog off the table. She carried him to a cage and gave him a dog cookie.

"You guys are wrong about Grace," Dink whispered. "She really likes animals."

"Lots of crooks like animals," Josh reminded Dink.

Ruth Rose nudged them. "Come on. Let's go watch Officer Fallon get fingerprints."

The problem was, there were none. Officer Fallon spread the dust, but no prints appeared. "Well, I guess he wiped the door or wore gloves," Officer Fallon said.

"Or she wore gloves," Josh muttered.

Dink remembered something else. "Mrs. Wong said there were tiny letters on the leg band," he said to the vet. "Did you read them?"

"I sure did, Dink. Come on inside and I'll show you."

Officer Fallon and the kids crowded into the office. Grace Lockwood was filling out some papers at the desk. Josh stared at her until Dink gave him a little shove.

"Hand me that leg band, would you, Grace?" the vet asked.

Grace nodded and gave the band to Doc Henry. The vet picked up a magnifying glass from his desk and handed it and the leg band to Dink. "Tell me what you see, young man."

Dink peered at the band through the glass. "Letters and numbers," he said.

"Can you read them?"

"'GLKS-6-17,'" Dink read. He looked up. "What does it mean?"

Doc Henry took the band and the glass.

"The letters are a mystery to me, but the numbers may be dates," he said. "If I'm right, the numbers mean Flash was born on 6/17-June 17th."

"Could the letters be the initials of the person who took Flash?" Josh asked.

"That's good thinking," Doc Henry said. "Those

letters could be initials. But whose?"

"Without any fingerprints," Officer Fallon said, "I'd say our thief has gotten away free as a bird!"

Dink stole a look at Grace. Her name tag stood out against her white jacket. Maybe the GL on the leg band stood for Grace Lockwood!

Dink gulped. Was Josh right? Was Grace Lockwood kidnapping falcons after all?

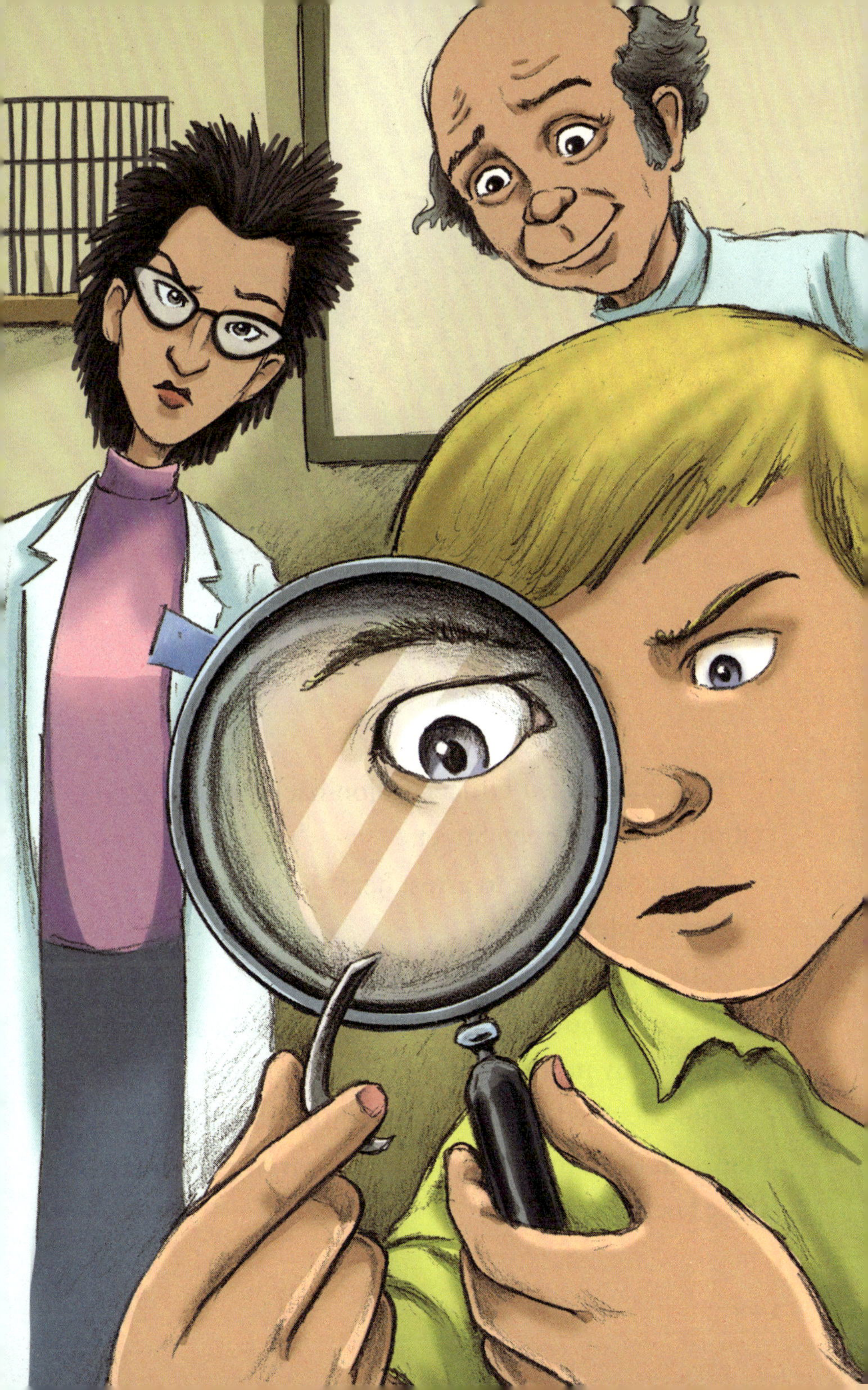

Chapter 10

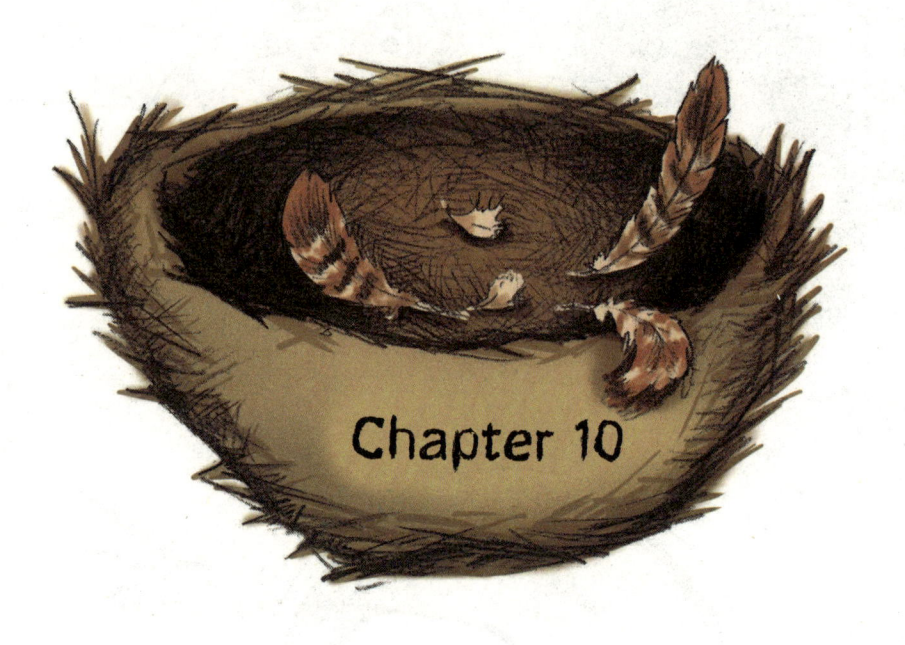

The kids walked Officer Fallon back to the police station on West Green Street.

"So are you going to arrest her?" Josh asked.

"Arrest who, Josh?"

"Grace Lockwood!" Josh said.

Officer Fallon smiled and shook his head. "We don't have any proof that she's done anything wrong."

Dink decided not to say anything about the GL initials on the band. Josh was already trying to throw Grace Lockwood in jail!

"Don't worry, Josh," Officer Fallon continued. "I'm sure we'll catch whoever's doing this."

The kids watched him walk into the station. "Come on," Dink said. "Let's go to the petting zoo for a while."

"Dink, don't you care about the falcons?" Josh asked.

"Sure I care. But you heard Officer Fallon," Dink said, crossing West Green Street. "We don't have any proof that it was Grace Lockwood."

Josh kicked at a stone. "Trust me, you guys. There's something weird about her!"

Dink laughed. "Josh, you just think she's weird 'cause she caught you staring at her cheeseburger!"

The kids cut around the library and entered the zoo. Llamas and baby deer nibbled pellets from kids' hands. A goose waddled along in front of six goslings. There were a few animals in cages, but most were loose.

Several teenagers walked around selling animal food. They wore dark green shorts and shirts with big round badges. The badges said GLPz, for Green Lawn Petting Zoo.

"Wait a sec, guys," Ruth Rose said. "I want to feed the fawn."

Dink and Josh watched her hurry over to one of the teenagers.

"Well, I still think Grace Lockwood's the one," Josh insisted. "We should tell Curt about her."

"Tell him what, that she gave you a dirty look?" Dink asked.

"For one thing, I'm gonna tell him about the initials on that leg band," Josh said. "He might know what they mean."

Ruth Rose came back with a small bag of pellets. "Want some?" she asked Dink and Josh.

"Better not give any to Josh," Dink said. "He might eat 'em!"............

"Haw haw," Josh said, taking a few of the pellets from Ruth Rose's bag.

They fed the deer and the llamas, then left the zoo.

Josh called Curt Striker's office from the lobby of the Shangri-la Hotel.

He hung up. "Not there."

游隼的羽毛

"Now what?" Ruth Rose said.

"Let's go to his cabin again," Josh said. "If he's not there, we can leave a note."

"Saying what?" Dink asked.

Josh dug a pencil out of his pocket. He got a piece of paper from Mr. Linkletter, the hotel clerk, and wrote on it.

"This," he said, showing the paper to Dink and Ruth Rose.

Dink stared at Josh. "What do you think GL

FOR CURT STRIMER:
FLASH'S LEG BAND HAS GLKS 6-17 WRITTEN ON IT. I THINK I KNOW WHAT THE GL STANDS FOR.
JOSH PINTO

stands for?" he asked.

Josh grinned. "Grace Lockwood!"

"But what about the KS?" Ruth Rose asked.

Josh shrugged. "That's what we'll ask Curt. Come on!"

The kids hiked up River Road to Bridge Lane. Halfway there, Ruth Rose suddenly stopped.

"What's the matter?" Dink asked.

She was staring into space. "Something's bugging me. It was something I saw at the DEP office, but I can't remember what!"

"Maybe it was that stuffed owl," Josh said. He made big owl eyes at Ruth Rose.

"No, I think it was something I saw on a desk." She stomped her foot in the dusty road. "Why can't I remember?"

A few minutes later, they reached Curt's cabin. Josh walked up and knocked on the door.

There was no answer.

"Guess he's not home," Dink said.

"Maybe he's in the backyard," Josh suggested. "Let's take a look."

The backyard was empty except for a pile of firewood.

Ruth Rose pointed to a dirt path that led into the woods. "Maybe this is how he got to the tree yesterday," she said.

Suddenly, they heard a low whistle.

"What's that?" Josh said.

"Just someone calling his dog," Dink said. "Come on, let's get out of here. We're trespassing."

The whistle sounded again. Josh started running up the path. "That's a falcon!"

Dink and Ruth Rose followed Josh. They found him standing in front of a small shed. On one side, a window flap had been propped open.

"Listen," Josh whispered.

The kids heard tweeting sounds and more whistles coming from the shed.

"There are falcons in there!" Josh said. He ran around the side and started tugging at a thick padlock on a door.

"Stupid thing is locked!" Josh said.

Ruth Rose went back to the window. "Boost me

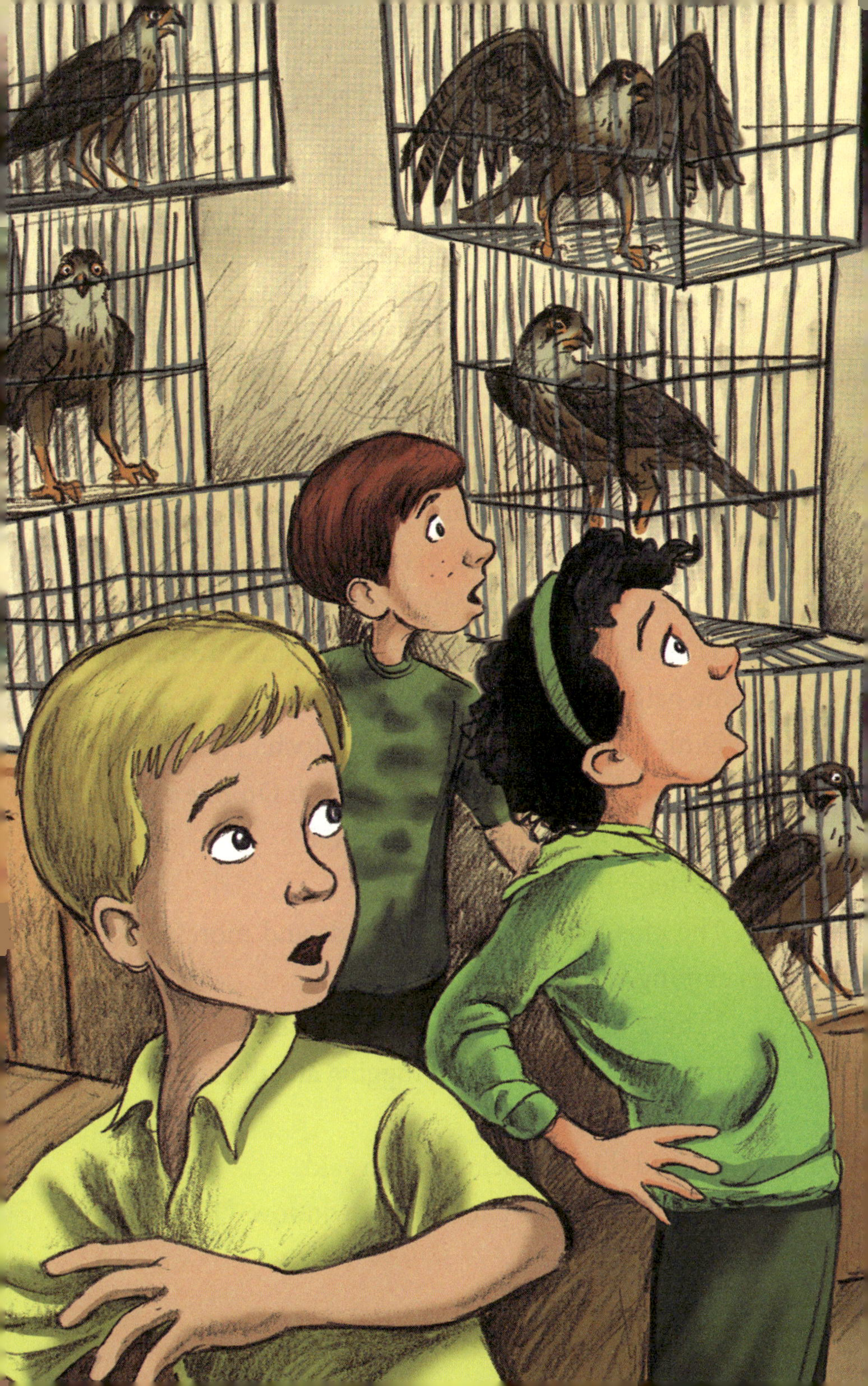

up, guys."

Dink and Josh crisscrossed their arms. Ruth Rose climbed on and hoisted herself up. "There are about ten cages in there filled with falcons!" she said.

Josh and Dink let her down.

"I'm going inside," Josh said.

"We're going with you!" Ruth Rose said.

A wooden barrel lay in the tall weeds a few yards away. The kids rolled it over and stood it under the window.

Standing on the barrel, Josh was able to crawl through the opening.

Ruth Rose went next. Then Dink.

The inside of the shed was cool and dark. In the dim light from the window opening, Dink counted at least a dozen falcons in cages.

The birds flapped their wings and let out low whistles. Their dark eyes watched the kids' every movement.

Suddenly, the light from the window was blocked. Curt Striker was glaring in at them!

"You brats just couldn't mind your own business!" he said. "You had to snoop, didn't you?"

Then his face disappeared. A moment later, the window flap slammed shut.

Chapter 11

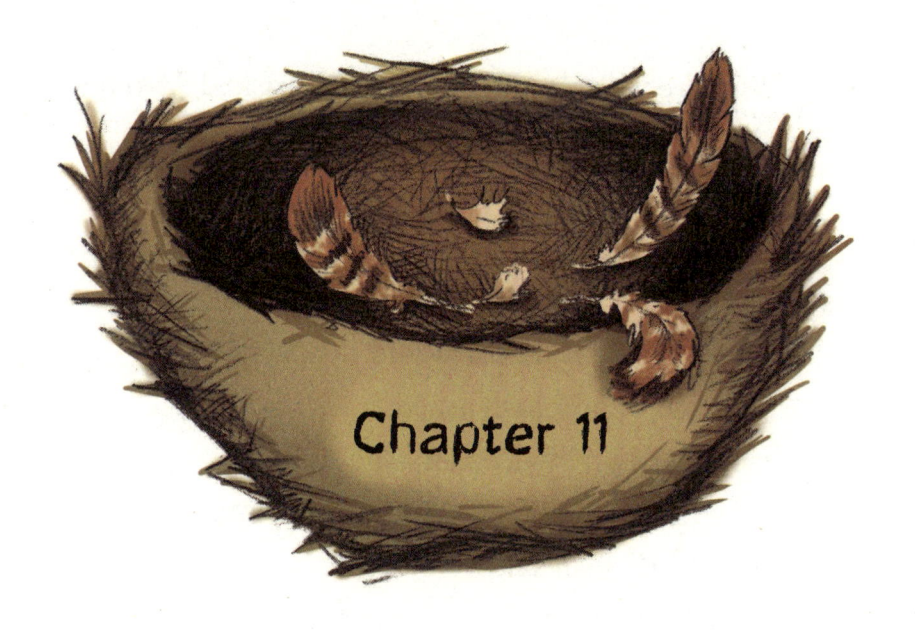

Dink stared at the spot where daylight had been. He could feel Ruth Rose and Josh come closer.

"What if he doesn't let us out?" Ruth Rose asked.

"Let's try to get that window flap open again," Dink said.

Dink and Josh hoisted Ruth Rose up to the window. She shoved against the flap. "Forget it," she said. "He must have locked it."

They tried pushing against the door, but it too was solidly locked.

"What're we gonna do, guys?" Josh asked. "No one even knows we're here!"

Dink walked around the dim shed, feeling the walls for openings. In one corner, he stumbled over some rakes and shovels.

"Guys, look!" Ruth Rose said suddenly.

"Look at what?" Josh asked.

"On the floor, by my foot," she said.

Dink looked down and saw a round spot of white.

"Sunlight!" Josh said.

They looked up. There was a small hole in the roof.

Dink ran to the corner and grabbed a shovel. "Maybe we can bust through!" he said.

Josh took a rake. Together, they tried to poke at the small hole.

"I can't reach!" Josh said.

"Some of these cages are empty," Ruth Rose said. "Maybe you could stand on them!"

Together, Josh and Dink dragged four cages over and made a platform. Standing on it, they found that they could easily reach the ceiling.

They smashed at the hole. After a few minutes, it was the size of a softball. Hunks of wood, shingle, and tar paper fell on their heads and shoulders.

Dink stopped to wipe his eyes.

"My arms are killing me," Josh said, sitting on the cages to rest.

"At least now we can see better," Ruth Rose said. She walked around, looking at the caged falcons.

"The cages all have labels," she said. "The first two initials are different, but the second two are always KS."

"Guys, I found Flash," Dink said.

He was looking at a cage holding three young falcons. The label on the cage door read GLKS-6-17.

"OH MY GOSH!" Ruth Rose yelled. "I just remembered what I couldn't remember!"

"What?" Dink asked.

"When we went to Curt's office, I saw a nameplate on his desk," she said. "His name is spelled with a K, not a C!"

"I don't get it," Josh said.

"I do," Dink said. "The KS on Flash's leg band

stands for Kurt Striker, right, Ruth Rose?"

"Right! And I bet the GL stands for Green Lawn!" she said.

"Now I get it," Josh said. "He labeled the falcons with the place he found them and his own initials."

"We have to tell Officer Fallon," Ruth Rose said.

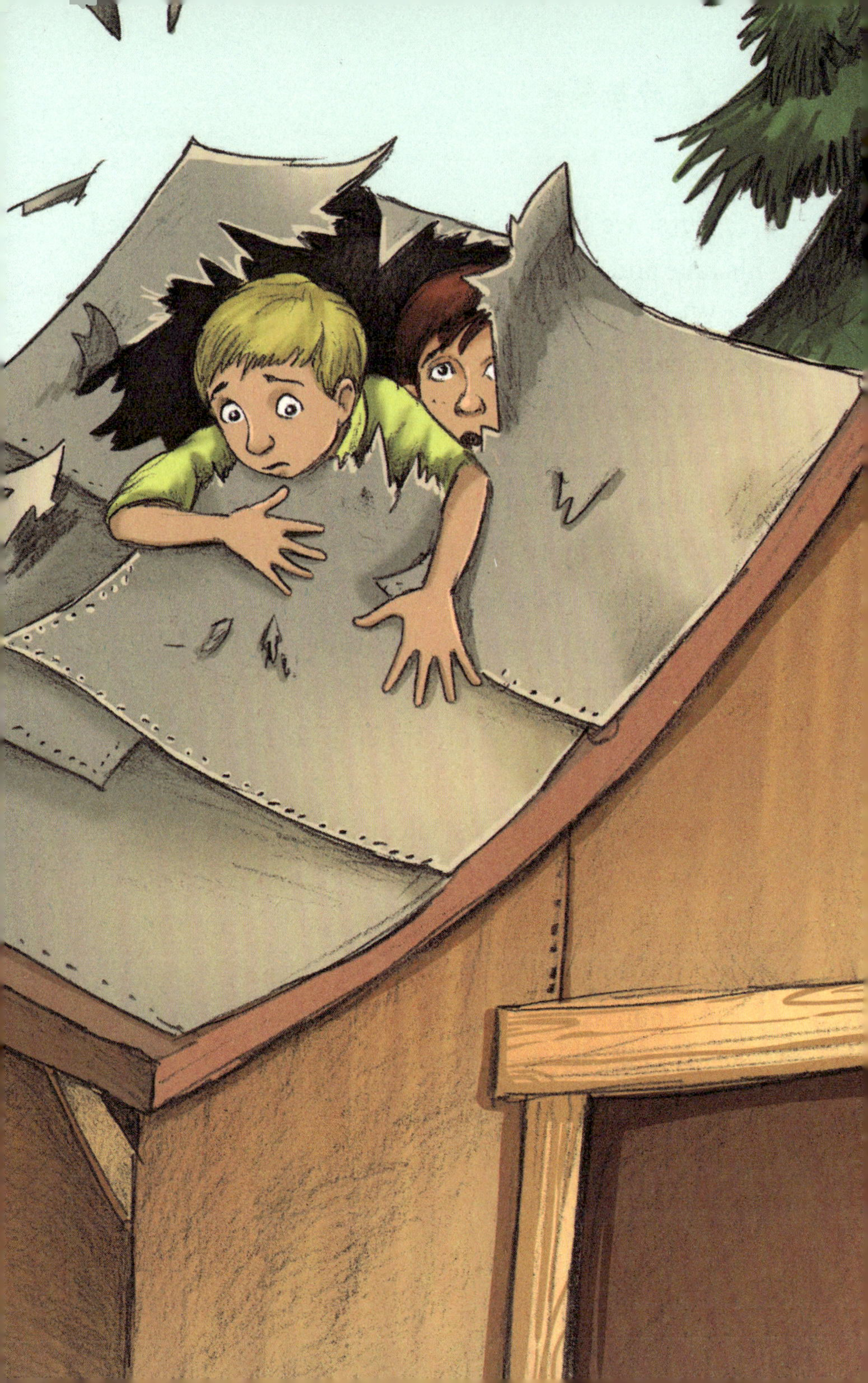

"First we have to get out of here!" Josh grabbed his rake and climbed back on the stack of cages.

With Dink and Josh both smashing at the roof, they made the hole larger. Sunlight poured in on their sweaty, dirty faces.

Finally, the hole was wide enough to crawl through.

"Pile up more cages!" Ruth Rose said.

With two more cages on the stack, the kids could climb out onto the shed roof.

They sat for a minute, breathing in the clean air and feeling the sun on their faces.

"It was him the whole time," Josh said, sounding disappointed.

"At least we found the falcons," said Dink.

Josh walked to the edge of the roof and looked down. "The barrel's still there," he said. "Come on, we can climb down."

As soon as they were on the ground, the kids ran toward Main Street and the police station.

Chapter 12

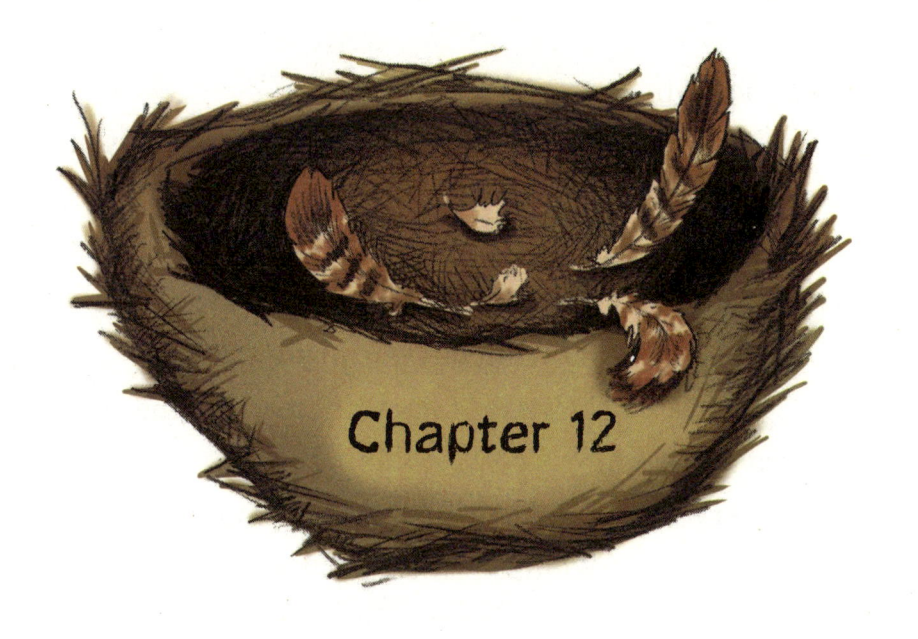

An hour later, it was all over. Doc Henry, Grace Lockwood, and Officer Fallon sat with the kids in a booth at Ellie's Diner.

"They caught Kurt Striker in Massachusetts," Officer Fallon said. "He's sitting in a jail in Springfield right now, waiting to be shipped back here."

"So he took the falcons from the nest?" Josh asked.

"Not only that nest, Josh," Grace Lockwood said. "He took birds from nests in three other states that we know of."

Doc Henry smiled. "I think we owe you kids an explanation," he said. "Grace isn't a vet. She's an undercover agent with the Department of Environmental Protection. She was assigned to Green Lawn for one reason:to keep an eye on our falcon population."

Josh stared at Grace. "I knew there was something weird about you!"

Everyone laughed. "Grace knew about the nest," Officer Fallon told Josh. "And she knew that you were out there a lot with your binoculars."

"I watched you watching the falcons," Grace said. "At first I thought you had taken them."

"You thought it was Josh?" Dink said. "He thought it was you!"

"I know," Grace said, smiling at Josh. "You kept looking at me funny!"

"Did you suspect Kurt Striker?" Ruth Rose asked.

Grace shook her head. "Not a clue. We have you kids to thank for figuring that out."

"So what was he doing with the falcons?" Dink asked.

"You kids were right about that one, too," Doc Henry said. "Striker had a little business going. He was taking young falcons and training them to race."

"What will happen to them?" Dink asked.

"We'd like to set them all free," Grace said. "But they've had a lot of human contact, so they probably wouldn't make it in the wild. Don't worry, there are plenty of wonderful zoos that keep animals happy and safe."

"Maybe Flash could live in the Green Lawn Petting Zoo!" Josh said.

"Now, there's a great idea!" Doc Henry said. "I'll talk to them about adopting all three from Flash's nest."

"As for Kurt Striker, he'll spend some time in jail," Officer Fallon said. "He'll no doubt rat on a few of his cronies, and they'll join him."

Ellie came over carrying a large tray. "Ice cream on the house!" she said. "I brought vanilla for every—"

"But I always get pistachio!" Josh said.

"You didn't let me finish, Josh," Ellie said.

"You'll have to excuse Josh," Ruth Rose said. "He

gets cranky when he's hungry."

"And he's always hungry!" Dink added.

"As I was saying," Ellie went on, "vanilla for everyone except Joshua Pinto, the boy who saved our falcons!"

She set a huge dish of pistachio ice cream in front of Josh. "And I want you to eat every bite," she said, smiling.

"Don't worry about Josh," Dink said. "That'll be gone in a flash!"

Text copyright © 1998 by Ron Roy
Cover art copyright © 2015 by Stephen Gilpin
Interior illustrations copyright © 1998 by John Steven Gurney
All rights reserved. Published in the United States by Random House Children's Books,
a division of Random House LLC, a Penguin Random House Company, New York.
Originally published in paperback by Random House Children's Books, New York, in 1998.

本书中英双语版由中南博集天卷文化传媒有限公司与企鹅兰登（北京）文化发展有限公司合作出版。

"企鹅"及其相关标识是企鹅兰登已经注册或尚未注册的商标。
未经允许，不得擅用。
封底凡无企鹅防伪标识者均属未经授权之非法版本。

©中南博集天卷文化传媒有限公司。本书版权受法律保护。未经权利人许可，任何人不得以任何方式使用本书包括正文、插图、封面、版式等任何部分内容，违者将受到法律制裁。

著作权合同登记号：字18-2023-258

图书在版编目（CIP）数据

游隼的羽毛：汉英对照／（美）罗恩·罗伊著；（美）约翰·史蒂文·格尼绘；刘巧丽译. -- 长沙：湖南少年儿童出版社，2024.10. --（A to Z神秘案件）.
ISBN 978-7-5562-7817-6

Ⅰ．H319.4
中国国家版本馆CIP数据核字第2024L3M783号

A TO Z SHENMI ANJIAN YOUSUN DE YUMAO

A to Z神秘案件 游隼的羽毛

[美] 罗恩·罗伊 著　　[美] 约翰·史蒂文·格尼 绘　　刘巧丽 译

责任编辑：唐凌　李炜	策划出品：李炜　张苗苗　文赛峰
策划编辑：文赛峰	特约编辑：杜天梦
营销编辑：付佳　杨朔　周晓茜	封面设计：霍雨佳
版权支持：王媛媛	版式设计：马睿君
插图上色：河北传图文化	内文排版：马睿君

出 版 人：刘星保
出　　版：湖南少年儿童出版社
地　　址：湖南省长沙市晚报大道89号
邮　　编：410016
电　　话：0731-82196320
常年法律顾问：湖南崇民律师事务所　柳成柱律师
经　　销：新华书店

开　本：875 mm×1230 mm　1/32		印　刷：三河市中晟雅豪印务有限公司
字　数：91千字		印　张：5.25
版　次：2024年10月第1版		印　次：2024年10月第1次印刷
书　号：ISBN 978-7-5562-7817-6		定　价：280.00元（全10册）

若有质量问题，请致电质量监督电话：010-59096394　　团购电话：010-59320018